DANCING
WITH

A MOTHER AND SON
WHO BROKE FREE

EMILY COLSON

PROLOGUE & EPILOGUE by
CHARLES W. COLSON

D1550295

ZONDERVAN

ZONDERVAN.com/
AUTHORTRACKER
follow your favorite authors

ZONDERVAN

Dancing with Max
Copyright © 2010 by Emily Colson and Charles W. Colson

This title is also available as a Zondervan ebook. Visit www.zondervan.com/ebooks.

This title is also available in a Zondervan audio edition. Visit www.zondervan.fm.

Requests for information should be addressed to:
Zondervan, *Grand Rapids, Michigan 49530*

This edition: ISBN 978-0-310-00019-8 (softcover)

Library of Congress Cataloging-in-Publication Data

Colson, Emily, 1958–
    Dancing with Max : a mother and son who broke free / Emily Colson ; with a
prologue and epilogue by Charles W. Colson.
      p. cm.
    ISBN 978-0-310-29368-2 (hardcover, jacketed)
    1. Colson, Emily, 1958– 2. Autism in children—Religious aspects—Christianity.
3. Mother and son—Religious aspects—Christianity.
I. Colson, Charles W. II. Title.
BV4910.5.C66 2010
248.8'63092—dc22
[B]
2010013102

Any Internet addresses (websites, blogs, etc.) and telephone numbers printed in this book
are offered as a resource. They are not intended in any way to be or imply an endorsement
by Zondervan, nor does Zondervan vouch for the content of these sites and numbers for
the life of this book.

Cover design: *Jeff Gifford*
Cover photography: *Emily Colson; signature by Max*
Interior design: *Beth Shagene*
Editorial: *John Sloan, Bob Hudson, and Elaine Schnabel*

Printed in the United States of America

12 13 14 15 16 17 /DCI/ 23 22 21 20 19 18 17 16 15 14 13 12 11 10 9 8 7 6 5 4 3 2 1

Thank you, Max

CONTENTS

EMILY, MAX, AND ME

Charles W. Colson

*D*ancing with Max is the story of my daughter, Emily, and her autistic son, Max. Emily is the author, and I am in an unaccustomed supporting role.

When I wrote *Born Again*, the memoir of my experiences in the White House, my conversion, and time in prison, I didn't think I'd ever be involved in such a deeply personal project again. That is, until now. I was not ready for the height and the depth of feeling I experienced as Emily unfolded her and Max's story in this book.

Emily and I share our perspectives of the joys and suffering we've discovered. I write mine in the book's prologue and epilogue, in which I talk about my relationship with Emily, the strength she gave me in my own life by watching what she's done in hers, and how Max came to make a bigger place in our hearts than anyone could ever imagine. Emily shares her moving story, of life's struggles but of its even greater victories, in her own words. She is a gifted writer.

This is a story of triumph, in spite of the suffering and pain. It is most of all a love story, and a story about changed lives — Emily's, Max's, and also mine.

CONFESSIONS
OF A DAD

CHARLES W. COLSON

The year was 1986. Arriving at Ninoy Aquino Airport in Manila, I was greeted by a large welcoming committee of Prison Fellowship International volunteers and workers wearing festive leis, some of which were immediately draped around my neck. Filipinos are among the most generous and gracious people in the world. This was my last stop on a whirlwind tour of the South Pacific. I had visited prisons in New Zealand and Australia and had spoken at the Australian national prayer breakfast before going on to prisons and a huge public gathering in Port Moresby, Papua, New Guinea.

Exhausted from my four-hour flight on Air Niugini, I was hoping for a few hours' rest. But it was not to be. My Filipino brothers and sisters had scheduled every minute of my three days in Manila.

On my second night in the hotel, I was awakened with stomach cramps. I was expelling blood. Alarmed, I called Nard Jimenez, a successful businessman in the Philippines and a good friend. He immediately came to my hotel, bringing with him a doctor, who was also a sympathetic Christian brother. Even though his specialty was urology, he was confidant that my hemorrhaging was most likely due to an ulcer. "We need to take you to the hospital immediately," he said. "Surgery may well be required."

You'd have to know Manila to understand my reaction. Millions of people, jammed together; hundreds of thousands living in the streets in tin huts in many parts of the city; and nonstop gridlock that makes any crowded expressway in America look like a country road. The only way to penetrate the traffic is with police escorts — either the real police or one of hundreds of private companies that escort the wealthy and powerful through Manila every day. This was early Saturday morning, when traffic would be at its worst. I had a big speech scheduled for that night, and I was booked to fly home the next morning. If I stayed in Manila, how could my family even get to me? Memories of Third World hospitals I'd seen gave me cold chills.

"What's the alternative?" I asked. The doctor told me I didn't have one. "You can bleed to death quickly," he added gravely.

"Medicine?" I asked, pleading.

"Once in a while it works," he acknowledged, "but I don't recommend it." He shook his head. He was smiling, but then, Filipinos always smile.

When I told him this would just have to be one of those "once-in-a-while" occasions, he scurried off and returned with bags of pills and antacid solutions. Then my friends left me so that I could sleep, but they promised to stand by in case I needed to be whisked to the hospital.

A few hours later when I awakened, mercifully (perhaps miraculously, I thought) the bleeding and pain had subsided. Though groggy from the medications, and against the stern advice of the doctor, who had returned, I rashly insisted on speaking that night. "I haven't come halfway around the world to disappoint a big crowd," I said with a weak pretense of bravado.

The doctor warned me that I was taking a big chance by flying home the next day. If the bleeding resumed on the flight, he warned, I could bleed to death in an hour or two. But I decided my chances were better on the flight than they would be in a Philippine hospital.

Ron Nikkel, president of Prison Fellowship International, who was traveling with me, made contact with friends in each of the cities where our flight stopped — in case we had an emergency. So Sunday morning I began a journey that took sixteen anxious hours but eventually got me home to Naples, Florida.

Immediately I was given an extensive examination. X-rays revealed a small ulcer, which for some unknown reason had stopped hemorrhaging. But the gastroenterologist didn't buy that diagnosis — which probably saved my life. "Ulcers just don't start and stop bleeding," he said.

So he ordered more tests. Even before they were complete, he informed me that he had discovered a tumor that had punched a hole in my stomach wall. It was a frightening diagnosis.

Thus began an experience that nearly cost me my life but gained my daughter back.

THE SURGERY THAT WOULD REMOVE THE TUMOR — and perhaps much of my stomach, depending on the results of the biopsy — was scheduled for January 1987 and was to be performed by the chief surgeon at Georgetown Hospital in Washington, D.C. I was given the treatment reserved for VIPs and government officials — not necessarily a good thing, I would soon discover — but it did mean a private room with a special anteroom right across from the nurse's station. The spacious accommodations would prove to be a good thing because my stay in the hospital was to be longer — much longer — than anticipated.

I told my sons, Wendell and Chris, both in their midthirties, and the baby of the family, my daughter, Emily, then twenty-eight, that I would be just fine, that this was simply routine surgery. They certainly didn't need to interrupt their schedules to travel to D.C.

My sons agreed, but Emily would have none of it. She flew to D.C. the night before the surgery and, along with my wife, Patty, was waiting for me as I was wheeled out of the recovery room after four hours on the operating table. I'd never known a more beautiful sight in my life than the smiling faces of the two women I most dearly loved. I knew from their expressions I was going to be all right.

"Cancer?" I asked. Still smiling, they nodded yes.

"Did they get it all?" I asked. Again they nodded, before I fell back into my narcotic-induced slumber.

Emily and Patty stayed in my room all night, as I groaned in pain, coming out of the anesthesia's aftereffects.

The next day, though the pain was great, compounded by an uncomfortable drainage tube inserted through my nose into my stomach, I began the recovery. I was at least comforted by the assurance that I'd be out of the hospital in five to six days. I talked Patty into going home so she could get a good night's sleep, but Emily refused and camped out again, huddled in an easy chair in my room.

On the third day, everything came undone. The drainage tube, it turned out, was kinked and had to be twisted around by the doctor, accompanied by his flock of six gawking interns. That was one of my most painful moments in the hospital. Later that day, my temperature shot up, alarming the interns who returned and prescribed massive IV injections of antibiotics. Once I was stabilized, both Patty and Emily went home for the night.

Soon after they left, however, I must have taken a serious turn for the worse because I was in and out of delirium and writhing in pain. My vital signs alarmed the nurse. I don't remember what happened, but soon the doctors surrounded my bed. Close to midnight the nurses called Emily and Patty and told them to return to the hospital immediately.

Sometime that night I peered through the fog and saw their encouraging smiles once more beside my bed.

Although I was in trouble medically, I had the strangest sense of peace as I came in and out of delirium. *Is this what's known as "dying grace,"* I wondered? The only thought in my head was, *Thank God I know Jesus Christ. If I die, I'll be with him.* I had no real fear except, perhaps, for the haunting question: *How could anyone not come to Christ? Everybody will be in this place sooner or later.* I thanked God quietly and tried to thank Emily and Patty as well, but I had difficulty forming words. Speaking took more energy than I had. Every time I would come out of the fog, there stood Emily or Patty or both, holding my hand.

Had I not been in good shape, having had a lot of exercise in the weeks leading up to the operation, I might not have made it. My ailment turned out to be a life-threatening staph infection.

I will spare you the details of the next horrific three and a half weeks because the important part of this story is what happened to my family and me. Emily stayed for eleven days without leaving the room, day or night. I wouldn't learn until much later how much of a sacrifice that was for her — or the tumultuous challenges that were about to confront her.

The nights were the toughest. I'd often wake up, hallucinating. "Emily," I shouted out one night, "you're growing whiskers!" Emily and Patty were there to comfort and calm me. When I gradually regained some control of my senses in the second week, I found I was engaging Emily in long conversations, often reflecting back on her life and mine. I didn't know where Emily stood with the Lord. She was well aware of what had happened in my life, and she had gone through some rebellious years. So I prayed with her frequently, and I could often see tears in her eyes as I did. I had the strong feeling God was working in her life in a powerful way. I told her in one of our middle-of-the-night conversations that I hadn't been the dad I should have been — those were in my pre-Christian life — but I wanted to be now. My first marriage had failed — or rather, I had failed, and the kids had paid the biggest price.

As Emily held my hand and wiped my face with cool cloths, my mind wandered to our lives together. I vividly remembered Emily's birth in 1958 and the unalloyed joy I felt holding this beautiful baby in my arms. My little girl. I'd never seen a more beautiful child — and she continued to be beautiful as a toddler, with her blond bangs bobbing over her forehead. Back then, in 1960, I was working as the administrative assistant for a senior U.S. senator, and I was helping him prepare for an uphill reelection campaign. In the evenings, for four long years, I was also earning a law degree. This meant that I would race from the senator's office to the local law school across town for two hours of classes — and I was always late. Then I would drive to our tiny suburban home, arriving about 10:00 p.m., just in time to quaff down some warmed-over dinner, kiss the sleeping kids, and descend to my basement office to file through papers and study intensely until 1:00 or 2:00 in the morning. Then I was up again at 6:00 a.m. to start the process over.

My service in the Marines had established the pattern. I was away for months on end for maneuvers or to quell a banana revolt in Guatemala. As an infantry officer, I had long days and often nights in the field with troops. I was on duty around the clock. My oldest son, Wendell, was born at Camp LeJeune, and I saw precious little of him — or for that matter of Chris, who was born two years later, just as I was starting law school. Our third child, Emily, came along midway through law school, just as I was being plunged into big-league politics.

My weekends were my only real chance to try to be a dad, that is, when I wasn't studying or on call for some important political event. Even then, in those precious few moments when I could be with the kids, the boys got most of the attention. Archaic though it sounds today, fathers back then bonded quickly with their boys and shared the same interests in sports, toy soldiers, and cars. Emily got the least attention. The truth is I had no real idea about what a father did.

After successfully managing the senator's reelection campaign and his surprise victory in 1960 — another around-the-clock job — I, then all of twenty-eight years old, was hooked. A driven man, I was determined to change the world, to bring my political skills to bear, to rise in power. Even as I was busy building a successful law practice, I imagined myself in the White House someday, really changing the world. By the time I was in my early thirties I had everything a person could expect; only later would I realize in moments of deep conviction that I had nothing that really mattered. Nor did I realize how much my family was made to suffer for my obsessive ambition.

My second marriage was in 1964 to Patty, who has been the most loving, supportive wife and partner in ministry all these years. After our marriage I made an effort to see more of the children, taking vacations together and frequent trips to Washington. Though I've always loved my children deeply, they never really had the attention they deserved. Patty was wonderful with them, however, taking them everywhere as I did the work of the Washington super-lawyer and politico. I was on the phone night and day with clients or political figures, even when the kids were with us. They simply never had my undivided attention.

In 1969, one dream came true. Then newly elected President Richard Nixon invited me to be his special counsel.

The White House years were thrilling and exciting for the family, meeting the president, front-row seats at the inauguration, playing in my elegant White House office. But for those four years I had even less time to be just a dad. My insensitivity to Emily continued. I was bored one day at a White House briefing, so I started making notes, composing a letter to Wendell and Chris about the joy of serving one's country, how I hoped one day they would join the Marines. I never thought about my daughter.

But through all of this, the children proved their mettle, especially when my world collapsed and I was embroiled in the Watergate scandal. They paid an especially heavy price, often being mocked by other kids. And one day the teacher in Emily's high school class spoke about what an evil man Charles Colson was.

Notwithstanding, the children were really there for us. Wendell, an oarsman for the Princeton crew, gave up the chance to row in Olympic trials in Europe in order to stay with Patty when I went off to prison. Chris came frequently as well, spending wonderful weekends with me in prison — that is, as wonderful as something could be under those circumstances. And Emily, then fifteen, wrote me every day, and sent me a painting, a landscape entitled *A Window from Prison*. She did it so I could imagine the outside world while incarcerated. (It remains on my office wall today, one of my most treasured possessions.)

At least I had the good sense to consult with the children when I was making important decisions. When President Nixon asked me to serve as his special counsel in the White House, I called Wendell, Chris, and Emily. I explained that it would mean a big pay cut, that they might in fact see even less of me, and that it would be a strain on all of us in the public glare. All three affirmed the decision to do it, however. Wendell's response was, "Do it, Dad. You will always regret it if you pass it up." He was right, though neither he nor I understood why that would be so. No one could imagine that it would lead to prison and a totally new and different life.

During Watergate I was offered an opportunity by the special prosecutor to plea bargain, in which I would testify against the president and be given only a misdemeanor, which would not affect my law license, nor result in prison. It was very tempting. Again I consulted the family, explaining that I would have to agree to give testimony against the president that wasn't true. Patty and all three kids stood firm. Emily summed it up during one visit. "If it isn't true, Dad, don't say it is." Undeserving though I might have been, I was blessed with a great family — kids who were incredibly mature for their age.

Emily came through again, strengthening me greatly at a time when I was under maximum pressure. She came to be with me in the week before sentencing. We tried not to talk much about prison or anything that would discourage us, but my heart was heavy. I was most concerned, I think, how the kids would view me. Would they have lost respect?

At the end of the week a few days before the sentencing, I took Emily to National Airport so she could board the flight home to her mother. I wanted to spare her the trauma of the courtroom scene. On the Jetway, I embraced her, told her how much I loved her, and then she turned to board. I asked her to come back and put both of my hands on her shoulders, gripping them tightly. As hard as it was, I had to ask her, "Emily, are you ashamed of your dad?"

"No!" she snapped, with an almost defiant expression. "I'm so proud of you, Daddy."

After she boarded the plane, I could hold it back no longer. It must have been quite a sight at National Airport to see the White House "hatchet man," tough guy, the former Marine captain, standing alone and crying unashamedly.

I was not a person ever to cry, but all that had changed that night in August 1973 when I was witnessed to by a friend; alone in my automobile after leaving his house I came under the deepest conviction of my own sins and failures, including how I'd fallen short as a dad. The tears flowed freely that night, cleansing tears that were washing over so many wounds and releasing pent-up pain. For the first time in my life I felt a real freedom. I cried out aloud to God that night on that quiet country road, alone — but of course not alone. Christ called me to himself, as I sat in that car, with tears freely flowing.

AND TEARS BEGAN TO FLOW freely after my surgery as well, as the memories flooded back, and I stared into Emily's eyes, filled with such love and compassion. Lying helpless in a hospital bed, I was comforted, the pain of surgery and infection eased, by her gentle, warm touch as she wiped my fevered brow. She had a rare combination, I was realizing, of quiet calming tenderness on the one hand and a tough-minded, fierce determination on the other. She was relentless in seeing that I got the care I needed. She and Patty were always there, listening to the doctors, giving them the reports. I discovered an inner toughness in my daughter worthy of the Marine lieutenant that I dreamed my boys would one day become.

Before that moment, I realized, I had never really known Emily. I'd always seen her as the baby of the family, to be protected. But I was incredibly insensitive, and our relationship was often strained.

Her teenage rebellion had been particularly stressful. Emily the artist concluded her dad was an unreconstructed and, of course, insensitive conservative. During her occasional emotional outbursts she would stomp off, slam the door of her room, and lock herself in. Or worse — as when Patty and I took her on a trip to Europe as her high school graduation present. We stopped off in a small French town near the Swiss border. Emily didn't like her room. So, unknown to us, she stomped out of the hotel and began to walk through the streets of the town. The two hours that Patty and I couldn't find her were as painful as waiting for the verdict the day that I was sentenced to prison. Half the time Patty and I were praying, half the time frantically racing through the streets looking for her.

How thoughtless I now realize I was. We discovered later that she was scared to death, and with good reason. Her room was at the far end of the hotel, with a bidet, something she'd never seen, prominently displayed beside the bed. I had expected Emily to be just like her more mature and independent older brothers. Instead, she simply needed my attention, my love.

It sounds politically incorrect, but in my generation a father's greatest concern was seeing his daughter happily married and starting a family. But I almost got her wedding off to a rocky start. At the rehearsal dinner I used an old gag line in my toast — a dad giving away his daughter to someone is like giving a Stradivarius violin to a gorilla. Everyone laughed loudly except the groom and his family. It was funny, but not too smart. When I walked down the aisle the next day, my mind was filled with dreams for Emily — a brood of children, a nice home in the suburbs, indulging her artistic bent if she so desired, all happiness and joy. Well, those dreams didn't come true. But what did come true was far greater.

THESE PRECIOUS BUT PAINFUL MOMENTS IN THE HOSPITAL were a turning point in our relationship and in my life. I had gained a whole new respect for Emily, seeing her no longer as a child but as a mature young woman. It was one of those rites of passage that all parents have with their kids, when they realize the tables have turned. Your kids are no longer as dependent on you as you are on them. A friend of mine said he had that feeling the first time his son picked up the check for dinner at a restaurant.

But it was more than that. I'd always loved Emily, but I discovered in the hospital that I loved her in a far deeper way. I always thought she needed me; now we needed each other. A bond was formed, the kind that often comes about only through shared suffering.

As we talked in the hospital, I made all kinds of promises. When this was over, I assured her, our life would be different. We would take trips together as a family. I even planned to charter a boat so Patty and I could sail off the Maine coast with Emily and her husband. I promised to take much more free time and enjoy the things I now realized were most important in life. I wanted to spend time with her children — when they came along. Talking about these dreams helped ease the agony of my recovery. A happy ending to this nightmare was in sight.

But it was not to turn out that way. Little did either of us realize how important our bond, forged in that hospital, would become. Emily would soon find herself thrust into the middle of a maelstrom — her character and the toughness I'd come to admire were put to the supreme test. Thankfully, our relationship deepened, so we were able to walk through her crisis together as a family.

I never expected that my daughter would have to go through so many struggles, pain greater than I went through with my surgery.

But just as I've seen in my own life, God can do amazing things through our weaknesses. God can turn around the most hopeless situation and reveal his good purpose. What happened to Emily — and to her beautiful son — was beyond anything I ever imagined for her — or for myself.

I'll let Emily tell you her story in her own words.

CHAPTER 1

CAR WASH

O kay, maybe I *was* a little rebellious — but whenever my dad reminds me of that, I usually look him straight in the eye and say, "I think I turned out remarkably normal ... *all* things considered."

I didn't exactly have your normal life experiences, although who has? At seventeen, I was shy, guarded actually, with the self-confidence of a gnat. Which is why on this particular day, with the lamination barely cool on my driver's license, my mom volunteered to lead me through my very first car wash. All my young rebellious nature would be required to do was to follow.

I watched as my mom's 1970s hatchback disappeared into the black hole of foaming spray. I gulped nervously as a burly attendant waved his arm, expecting me to drive my eight-inch-wide wheels into four-inch metal tracks. Did he understand that I couldn't *see* my wheels? As I pulled forward it sounded as if my tires were screaming at me, the rubber screeching against metal. The attendant signaled me to stop.

I cranked down the window of my boxy old Plymouth Valiant. "Regular wash, please," I said, trying to act cool.

"Hands off the wheel. Foot off the brake. Keep it in neutral," he ordered, pocketing my money.

That's it? I thought. *Just sit here?*

My car jerked forward, and a frothy wave of water slapped against the windshield. As I was swallowed into the dark hole, I could see huge blue towels lapping tongue-like across my hood. It was such a Jonah-in-the-whale experience that even my feet felt wet. And then I looked down.

Apparently, the tattooed attendant had neglected to inform me that I should close the vents on my car, that ingenious 1970s pre-air-conditioning cooling system of little doors beside your ankles. The fact that these vents also blew leaves and road debris into your car tells you how closely this technology mimicked that of the Flintstones'.

There at my feet, gushing through these open vents with hydrant force, was enough water to fill an ocean.

I jammed my foot up against one of the vents but couldn't close it. The water pressure was too great. I pictured myself reaching the exit of the car wash with the interior of my car completely filled with water, like a rolling aquarium. And there I'd be, treading water with my lips stuck to the inside of the roof, sucking out the last bit of oxygen.

With survival at stake, there was only one thing to do: I put my hand on the wheel, threw it in reverse, and hit the gas. With an enormous crack the steel bar that held my car in place snapped. I flew backward, out of the entrance of the car wash, as though I'd been shot out of a whale's blowhole. Oddly enough, the attendant was not as relieved as I was to see me back where I'd started, safely on dry ground.

"Whaddaya doin'?" he screamed in his Boston accent, as he held the sides of his head. "Ya broke my cahwash."

I thought it best not to ask for my money back and did the only logical thing a seventeen-year-old could think of — I drove away as fast as possible.

When I pulled around the corner, my mom was waiting. She rolled down her window and watched as I opened my car door, releasing a splat of sudsy water against the pavement. I waved my hand, motioning for her to drive away, and yelled, "I'd rather wash it myself."

That was many years ago, and I haven't backed out of a car wash since. But I have felt exactly the same way: the challenges ahead looking just as threatening, just as ominous. Pressure is rising and I can see the end. I'm sure I'll run out of oxygen, that I can't possibly survive.

But I *have* survived.

CHAPTER 2

STARING AT THE WALL

There is no ordinary day in our lives, my autistic nine-year-old, Max, and me.

This morning my son, who hadn't slept all night, defiantly refused to get out of bed. I knew that if he sensed for a second that I was upset, I'd lose him to a tantrum. So I had to stay calm and happy-faced no matter what, no matter how exhausted I felt. But the rest of the world lives by the clock, so I did the impossible. I swung from a trapeze, stuck my head into the mouth of a lion, did the work of twelve burly men, and voilà, my son was ready for school, fresh as a daisy.

An hour later the school called me. "He's really having a rough time. You need to come down here and get him." So I jumped into the car as if I'd been struck by lightning and rushed back to Max.

At the school I was greeted with the hospitality one might extend to the Unabomber, as if I had some evil plot to ruin the teachers' and administrators' lives. They acted as if I had hidden the remote control and enjoyed watching them struggle to figure out my child without it. Max had done so well in public school the year before. But it was clear they could no longer meet his needs, and I wanted some accountability. So now I was just as much a problem for them as Max. I walked down the dark hallway to find my son sitting against the wall, closed down, afraid, with several teachers watching. I threw my arms around him and held him. I desperately wanted to protect him, to cover him with a layer of love so impenetrable that even the harshest judgments couldn't touch him. When he was ready, I slid my hand into his, and we left together without looking back.

I'd missed my chance to go to the pharmacy while Max was at school. Now he would have to come with me. *I'll make it work this time*, I told myself, as if just wishing it could establish some authority over his autism. It was easier when he was younger, when I could push him in his stroller or contain him in a shopping cart. But at nine he was just too big. These past few months had been his first brush with freedom, and it had tested us both. It must be overwhelming for him, all these lights and sounds and people. He can't make sense of it, of what he's supposed to do. Ordinary life comes at him like a 747. He's counting on me to help him, guide him, to act as his air-traffic controller. But I'm learning too.

Max handled the first few minutes in the pharmacy beautifully, but soon he was darting up and down the aisles. So I scooped him up as if I were King Kong and carried this gargantuan nine-year-old to the prescription counter. Really, there should be a special checkout line for people holding twice their body weight in squirming offspring. I had these huge biceps, the trophies of a single mother, like guardrails wrapped around my son. But we were okay. We were managing.

Until Max found a toy that played music. He pushed the button and the song started. His face began to grimace and his back arched. I watched fear travel through his bloodstream like an injection. He desperately tried to turn the music off, but the toy had to play the whole song from beginning to end — or until someone put it out of its misery. Max picked it up and started smashing it until the batteries spilled across the floor. I tried to intervene, pulling away the toy.

"Let's go Max. Mommy has something really fun to do next," I pleaded in my happiest voice, trying to bribe him toward the car before he blew. But it was too late. He threw himself on the floor and started to kick and writhe. It's not the kind of tantrum other kids have, putting up a fuss when they want to buy something. What Max wants is for the world to make sense, to feel safe, and it doesn't.

This toy was just one more thing he couldn't control in his whirling, chaotic world.

I knew what was ahead. It was almost a routine at this point, and it was why I needed to get to the store before Max came home. He would cry and scream, and then he would don his fatigues and set out on a mission to seek and destroy all the bad noise-making things in the store. I was sweating, trying to change the course of history, but he was already programmed like a Navy SEAL.

It's remarkable how quickly space clears around you when your autistic child explodes in public. I tried not to care about the people staring at us, to keep my focus on helping Max. I tried not to lose an ounce of energy to humiliation. I poured sweat, all those stifled tears that find their way out, and called to a clerk who was hiding behind the checkout counter, like a soldier ducking into her foxhole.

"Can you get the manager? Please."

A minute later a sweet young girl — the manager — cautiously approached us and looked down at me with big doe eyes. I didn't have time for this. "I need a big guy. Is there a big guy here?" I yelled to her as I knelt across my child, trying to keep him from getting up and running into customers, swiping the shelves clear of the neatly stacked potions.

She came back with a young man who wasn't exactly big. I needed Hercules, but he would have to do. He looked as if he wished he'd called in sick that morning. He took Max under one arm and I took the other, and we got my son, still kicking and screaming, into the car.

I crawled into the driver's seat, locked the doors, and slumped my head against the steering wheel. Love and hate and helplessness and fear consumed me. My heart was pounding. My heart was breaking. And it was only noon.

That night, when Max was in bed, I found my way to the living room and fell into the rocking chair. There was nothing left of me. My legs hung over the edge like broken tree limbs, and my body sunk as if it were in quicksand. The phone rang, and I heard my chipper voice floating toward me from the answering machine. "We can't come to the phone right now, but if you'd like to leave a message…" Someone wanted me to talk.

Don't move, breath slowly, I reminded myself; it hurts less. I rubbed my fingers along the arms of my rocking chair as my eyes settled on the blank living room wall. I'd worked so hard on this house, painstakingly plastering my own walls, making them flat and even, like some sort of therapy, painting them the color of sunlight to bring something bright into our lives. This yellow wall was so familiar now, faithfully there at the end of each day, smooth and quiet, and asking nothing of me. For the past month it had been my closest friend, my refuge. Once Max was in bed, I could come downstairs and find it, exist there, let it wash over me like white noise. I wanted to become the emptiness of flat yellow. I wanted to stop feeling.

I don't know if it would be easier if I'd had a husband to help. There wasn't much left of me to offer another person. My family and friends are wonderful and help in every way they can, in every way they know, but at the end of the day it's just Max and me. And this thing called autism.

Max would be awake again soon, maybe in an hour, maybe in a few hours. I should sleep while I have the chance, before Max wakes up reciting videos for an hour — or two or three hours. But sleep meant doing something, and I was too exhausted to do anything. Maybe Max was awake, trying to make sense of the world, something I couldn't help him with. I didn't understand life right now any-more than he did. It would be easier if I had a guarantee that everything would get better, if I knew the struggle might even end at some point. It could end like trials do for other people, everyone gathering around celebrating, throwing a party with hors d'oeuvres and cake. Everyone noticing. But that wouldn't be our story. Tomorrow I would have to find the courage, the endurance, to breathe deeply and simply start again, even if no one noticed.

Most of the time we're great. I love Max desperately, as if my body were being turned inside out. It's an unquenchable love that takes up most of my existence. Max is not a burden; he is my greatest gift. I'm not about to give up. I'm just not sure I can keep going.

Do you see this, God? I know you're watching. I know you're in this, but we're at a dead end. Our problems don't have solutions. I've tried every intervention, and still Max is severely disabled with autism. He's not one of the kids who recovered, who gets cured. And I'm not sure I can recover from my wounds either. God, I don't understand. Why would you bring us this far, sustain us, provide for us, carry us through a war zone, if it was only to end here — a place without hope? I don't even know what to pray for anymore.

The phone rang again, calling to me in my rocking chair, trying to jar my gaze from the blank living room wall. But I just couldn't talk. There wasn't anything to say. Today had been like so many other days lately, and I was hanging on by a thread.

CHAPTER 3

DESIGNING MAX

I sat there staring at the same yellow wall for an hour, maybe more. This rocking chair was only nine years old but already showing signs of wear. As I ran my fingers along the armrests, feeling the rough oak grain under the varnish, I thought back to the first time I sat in it. The chair had been so smooth and shiny; life was smooth and shiny then too. My belly was huge, as if I was about to give birth to a torpedo. This wasn't just any rocking chair, the salesman reminded my husband, Garry, and me. It was a Kennedy rocker, the kind President Kennedy used in the oval office and at the family compound in Hyannis Port in the 1960s, with a sturdy oak frame and hand-woven rush seat and back. It was more than just comfortable; it conjured images of thick-haired, handsome men wearing billowy white cotton shirts and tossing a football on the beach. It spoke of being born into privilege.

We bought this chair as part of the truckload of equipment we assembled for the arrival of this tiny new life. Picking out bouncy seats, musical mobiles, and fancy furniture was just something to distract us, make us think we were still in control of our lives. Did we actually think a baby would care that we bought the high-end German-engineered, turbo-charged stroller? Garry and I were both working then and had plenty of money to shop with reckless abandon.

After a successful day's shopping we stopped for dinner at a favorite restaurant. My belly was so cumbersome that I could hardly

straddle the stool while we waited for a table. Not one of my more dignified moments — very pregnant and belly up to the bar. I squeezed
the lime into my club soda as the sound of blenders, mixing frozen
margaritas, roared in the background.

I loved being pregnant, keeping my baby safe and close to me, the
way you tuck your passport under your clothes in a foreign country. I loved everything about my life then — my husband, my career,
my home. But unless I wanted to give birth to a forty-pound toddler, things were about to change. We knew it was a boy, and we had
already named him Maxwell Charles.

Garry was getting curious about Max. So as we sat in this crowded
restaurant, with the mariachi band playing over the speakers, he
began choosing characteristics from an à la carte menu of desirable
family parts. By the end of his recipe he had created another Einstein,
who would partake in a least one, if not two Olympic Games. It was
endearing, but I was just the teensiest bit preoccupied with the whole
impending birth thing.

I couldn't imagine who Max would be. Everyone in my family
is unique. We have the brainy, the creative, the outgoing, the intro-
verted, the funny, the serious. I could only envision one thing: we
would be mother, father, and child all together. My parents divorced
when I was so young that I never knew what it was like to have a
whole family, one that wasn't separated by distance. This wasn't just
Max's chance. It was mine.

It hadn't been easy arriving at this ethereal moment of perfection.
We'd been through our own marital waves, Garry and me. Actually, we'd surfed a tsunami. We'd been married just five years when I
became curious about God and started reading the Bible. I was capti-
vated. And then, in the very next breath, life crashed over us with the
loss of two family members and my dad's surgery, which resulted in
infections and complications. The crisis magnified every unexplored
vulnerability in our relationship. Garry and I weren't strong enough
to take the wave, to pull together, and we separated for a year. It was

a devastating time. I didn't think I'd survive, but I did. We did. And now we were starting a family.

I WAS COMPLETELY UNQUALIFIED to take care of a baby. I'd never even changed a diaper. But a sudden bout of premature labor plucked me out of my job as creative director and landed me on four weeks of bed rest, which was ample time to obsess over every how-to baby manual available to mankind. When I picked up the phone to order the set of instructional videos on how to give a baby a bath, my mom stepped in like it was a drug intervention. "You don't need that, Emily. You're going to be okay without it." She'd been through this baby thing three times and had raised my two older brothers and me as a single parent from the time I was only five years old, but I was sure there must be new information by now, more updated soaping techniques that required extensive study. My final exam could be at any moment. And it was.

We rushed to the hospital on a Friday night, but they turned us back. Apparently, there is some clause that states if a woman is smiling, she isn't in labor. They didn't get it. I was always smiling. My nickname in grade school was Smiley-Emily. When we returned the next day, desperate for help, I gave Nurse Ratched my best James Dean scowl and we were in. It was time. But, once in the delivery room, Max had second thoughts. He wasn't dropping into position but was hiding way up under my rib cage. I could picture him hanging on to my ribs like monkey bars at a playground, refusing to let go. "No, Mom, just five more minutes." But the atmosphere was quickly changing. We didn't have more time. Max's heart rate was slowing down. Doctors and nurses started bustling around me like fry cooks in a busy restaurant kitchen, barking out commands. I felt so completely out of control, wanting answers but consumed with managing the pain. "Is he okay?" I kept asking the doctor. The nurses in their green cotton scrubs floated in and out of my view, reassuring me that everything was okay. The baby was fine.

They began prepping me for an emergency C-section, but a hospital protocol prevented my baby, who was now in fetal distress, from being delivered. The doctor was frantic, checking the heartbeat, trying to keep me calm, calling for the second anesthesiologist. It was two days before Christmas and my own obstetrician had already left for vacation. Between panting and screaming through unmedicated labor pains, I somehow mustered this out-of-body, I-brake-for-vanity moment and quite calmly asked the doctor if he could please do a bikini incision. I didn't want a huge up-the-middle scar you sometimes get in an emergency. I must have sounded like I was ordering from the Starbucks drive-thru in the middle of a war zone. And could I have a latte with that enormous incision? He nodded yes, and gave me a twisted little smile, probably trying to block out the image of my gigantic whale body covered by only four inches of fabric. Then the next wave of pain hit. "Get the baby out," I screamed. Heart rates were going down, tempers were going up.

Finally, they were ready. The doctor told my husband to leave. Garry looked down at me, his eyes wild and bloodshot. I didn't know he was afraid until that moment. I gripped his arm as he walked away, "Pray. Please, pray." I breathed in anesthesia like cool ocean air and was gone.

"Emily ... Emily ... you have a boy," I heard someone call while my eyes were still shut. You mean we lived? We made it? I was cold and shaking. Everything was so calm now, so strangely quiet. I opened my eyes to see the nurse passing an oversized red Christmas stocking to Garry. As he lay the stocking next to me I could see Max's head peeking out of the top. I gazed at him, stunned by the reality of his existence. He was beautiful, translucent, with little wisps of strawberry blonde hair and showing off the most impressive Elvis-like sideburns grown just for his debut. "Hi, baby Max," I smiled, reaching for him, brushing my hand against his cheek for the first time. But before I knew it, I was out again.

When I was a little more awake, I saw the very first photograph of Max, taken while I was still in the operating room. Garry was cradling this little mollusk, just minutes old, wrapped in a blanket with only a scrunchy pink face peeking out. Max's eyes were open, and his fingers stretched out like he was so surprised to be here. I was envious that I'd missed it, this moment we would always remember. But when I held that photograph and saw those first breaths of Max's life taken from his father's arms, I was sure Garry would never let him go. After all we had been through, life was finally falling into place.

IF LIVING IN THE SUBURBS AND DRIVING a Volvo qualified one to be a good parent, I would have been all set. But in those first few weeks after Max was born I felt like I'd landed on another planet. It didn't help that I'd been through more hours of labor than anyone who'd lived to tell about it, and had then delivered my child like a human Pez dispenser. I was, shall we say, a little sore. I called the hospital on the third day home hoping they could tell me where to find Max's off switch — or at least the volume control. Unfortunately, they remembered Max. "We couldn't get him to stop crying either," the nurse laughed. And then, of course, there was that first bath. Even those training videos couldn't have spared the trauma of holding on to a squirming, slippery infant in the kitchen sink when someone in the back bathroom flushed the toilet and my sink sprayer turned from warm water to boiling.

My husband, on the other hand — now, this man could diaper. He was like a rodeo cowboy diapering a young colt while holding on to a bucking bronco, one eye on his campfire checking that his beans didn't burn. How did he know this stuff? Why was he so confident while I handled Max like he was bread dough, trying to catch body parts before they dripped off?

That first morning alone in the house, after everyone went home and Garry went back to work, I sat holding Max in our new Kennedy rocker. He was so pink and frail, like a sea creature pulled from its shell. I watched an endless scroll of huge white snowflakes falling outside the window. I mentally factored how many hours it would be before my husband came home. Ten minutes went by. Twenty minutes. The past nine months — well, eight, because Max was in a hurry — had been so frenzied. Our friends and family had been so excited that after ten years of marriage we were having a baby. I had wanted to wait until I felt old enough, wise enough to handle anything. So why, my first time alone with Max, did I feel as if I were still a child? I held Max awkwardly as he slept in my arms, and I rocked.

But everything changed for me when Max was two weeks old. Garry and I were sitting against the pillows of our bed. Our baby, as usual, was crying with this huge open mouth, which looked like a big black kidney bean. He cried so much that he already had worry lines between his eyebrows like a smoker. Max was in Garry's arms, and I looked on as if our son were a science project and it was our job to determine what experiment might stop the tears. I was still working on book knowledge when, quite suddenly, an unexpected warmth came over my body. Max wasn't waiting to see if I could figure him out and pass the quiz. He had no idea that his mother was dreadfully ill equipped. All he needed was for us to help him, love him, mistakes and all. Without thought, I reached over and lifted Max from my husband's arms. I held him close and gazed into his little red tear-soaked face and softly said, "It's okay, Max. It's okay."

Garry stared at me and asked with a note of sarcasm, "What just happened to you?"

I didn't know it then, but at that moment, I fell in love with Max. I fell in love with all of it. We were a family.

CHAPTER 4

GROWING UP IN THE CLOUDS

Garry and I met in college when I was eighteen, back when I was certain that someday I'd be living as an artist in Soho, back when having children was the last thing on my to-do list. We were at a fraternity party where some very nice boys were throwing a television off the roof. I assumed the other freshman students — the ones who read the books and did the assignments — just hadn't heard about the parties. I didn't get serious about studying art until the next year, and thanks to the grace and patience of my parents, there actually was a next year. Unfortunately for me, there were no class offerings in how to blend in and be normal.

When I arrived at college, Watergate, and therefore my dad, seemed to be the biggest news story since the discovery of fire. I remember standing in line to register for classes and eagerly introducing myself to the girl standing beside me. "Hi," I said, hoping she'd be my first new friend. "I'm Emily."

The girl giggled helplessly. "I *know* who you are," she said. "I mean, we *all* know." I turned around to see every student behind me staring, some leaning out of their place in line to get a better look. "Everyone on campus knows you're coming," she added. "I found out last spring."

There was an awkward silence; she never told me her name.

I'D GROWN UP IN A SMALL Massachusetts town in one school system. People in my high school remembered when I'd been a goofy kindergartner adorned with a barrette the size of a hamster. They saw me go through my awkward adolescent years of wearing my brother's baggy sweaters every day and refusing to button the cuffs on my sleeves because it might look like I was trying too hard.

While most of my kindergarten classmates in the 1960s had never been on a plane, a mode of transportation typically used by businessmen only, my two older brothers and I became frequent flyers as we traveled to visit our dad and stepmother, Patty, in Washington, D.C. My parents divorced when I was just five, long before my dad became a Christian. Wendell and Chris and I would suit up in our Sunday best and sit in the bulkhead, guzzling free Cokes, while the flight staff kept an eye on us. We were crazy with the midair freedom, being pinned with junior-pilot wings and eating food that resembled Swanson TV dinners. I'd sneak away to the bathroom to admire the tiny individually wrapped soaps that popped out of a dispenser. They were pink. And apparently free. All fifty of them fit perfectly down the sides of my boots. The three of us floated in this state of wonder, suspended at thirty-three thousand feet, flying from one parent to the other.

When we landed in Washington our dad would make sure we saw all the sights and learned about the places "where all the great decisions are made," as he would tell me. We'd have private tours of the White House and the Capitol and the U.S. Mint. Doors were opened to us. Patty would often be our good-humored tour guide while our father was working. And everywhere we went we were preceded by the words, "These are Chuck Colson's kids." When Dad took a position with President Nixon, he would bring us to the annual White House Christmas party and to see performances at the Kennedy Center from the president's box. He brought me into the Oval Office when it was empty one day and let me sit behind the president's highly polished desk. I don't think I took up half the chair. My dad watched from the other side of the desk standing at attention like a marine. But I'm sure his eyes didn't sparkle when he looked across that same desk at the president.

The first time my dad introduced me to the president I actually thought my hair was standing on end. I must have been just fourteen. My dad had told me to call him "Mr. President," and I was sure it was one of my father's many practical jokes. The wisdom of my years told me to call the president by his real name, Mr. Nixon. But it didn't matter; when the president shook my hand I froze. My lips didn't work. I said absolutely nothing. As it turned out, the president was gracious enough not to mention my light-socket hairdo.

If any of this special treatment might have gone to our heads, it was quickly balanced when the plane landed back home in Massachusetts. Wendell and Chris and I lived with our mom, where our toys resembled the contents of an appliance-store dumpster, because that's where we got our best stuff. It's not that we couldn't afford toys; we lived in a lovely home in an affluent suburb of Boston. Our mom simply believed that prefabricated toys were "the last resort of a vacant mind." Her father had been a brilliant inventor. So she would give us all the cardboard, tape, glue, paint, tools, and motors we could wish for. She even agreed to let Wendell build an addition onto our home. He was thirteen at the time.

But our mother didn't let us run wild; she had rules. Regarding the full-sized trampoline in the middle of our living room, for example, the rule was that you could only bounce on your knees, your bottom, or, for those truly gifted such as my brother Chris, your stomach. If you broke the rule your head would poke through the plaster ceiling, which was definitely frowned upon. And Mom's rule for bringing all the furniture into the front yard was, "If you can carry it, you can build with it." She had her work cut out for her, raising three children by herself, but we never would have known that.

As we grew older, we would board the plane again, sans junior-pilot wings, to visit our dad after his painful prison sentence was broadcast as a television news flash interrupting the regularly scheduled programming. On one of these visits, when Dad was being held at a secure facility for witnesses testifying in major trials, a former army barracks, Patty and I were allowed to eat dinner with him in the mess hall. My dad and the other twenty inmates, primarily mafia informants, each took turns cooking dinners. It was dark and cramped and uncomfortably silent. Our square table was so tiny that our shoulders touched. We struggled to make conversation.

"Eat your food, Emily," my father instructed as he watched me slide a potato across my plate like a hockey puck in a puddle of yellow grease.

"I'm not hungry," I responded.

My dad looked at me with laser-beam eyes, "Don't offend the cook," he said under his breath. "You need to eat the food."

And back I would fly to Massachusetts, a little more grown up each time I would soar through those shifting clouds at three hundred miles an hour. And when I'd land back home, and return to my little world of high school, no one stared or asked me questions. Few even singled me out, except one girl. She was new to the school.

It was during Watergate when the story broke onto the front page of every newspaper that my dad had become a born-again Christian. This new girl made a beeline across the entire length of the high school cafeteria and started to speak before she'd even reached my spot at the lunch table. "Which life do you have?" she demanded, pointing at a little book with two black-and-white diagrams. I took a look. It wasn't exactly an SAT question. I pointed to the diagram with me in the center surrounded by concentric circles that contained everything else in the world. "And which life do you want to have?" she asked, peeking at me through her round wire-rimmed glasses. It didn't take me long. I mean, how much of a heel would I be to think I should be at the center? So I pointed to the diagram with God in the center. I'd never thought about it that way, but it was common sense. Her eyes bugged out and her body jolted like the conveyor belt she was riding just stopped abruptly. Apparently I had answered in a way that made her ask if we could find an empty classroom to talk, which made me feel uneasy and a little embarrassed. There, she read a few things from the book and prayed for me. I'm sure she told me what I was supposed to do next, but I really didn't realize what I'd just done. I'd said yes, and I meant it. But it would be years before I understood. And it certainly didn't happen that first year away in college.

My freshman year in college resembled the freedom I felt midflight as a little girl, untethered and completely independent, with my feet firmly planted in the clouds. One warm evening, as Garry and I sat on the granite steps below a towering stone building on campus, I casually mentioned how friendly the school felt.

"The administration is so nice here," I mulled, expecting him to tell me that niceness was simply customary in the Midwest. He gave me a curious look. "Ya know," I went on to say. "The way they stop at your dorm room every month to check on you and make sure you have everything you need?"

Garry looked down and started to snicker. I knew he was going to tell me something, but I thought he was so handsome that I didn't mind waiting. He scuffed one foot along the granite steps scratching pebbles under the sole of his shoe. He finally looked back at me.

"Who comes to your door, Emily?"

"The ... dean of students."

"Are you kidding?" he asked, with his eyebrows furrowed.

I didn't know how to answer, so I kept staring back at him.

He waited a moment, looked down at his feet once more before angling his face toward me with a half grin. "They don't do that for anyone else, Emily," he said. "They're only doing that for you."

We married right out of college and landed in a Norman Rockwell moment in a postcard-perfect New England town with gray-shingled houses, white wooden churches, and a breathtaking coast. Not exactly Soho. It was ten years before I considered having children. I was surprisingly happy, slipping comfortably into married suburban life, the kind of *normal* life I assumed other people had. The kind of normal that shifts as quickly as the clouds.

CHAPTER 5

SKYLIGHT BOY

Ten years of married life was certainly far from perfect, but it had all come together when the baby arrived. And fortunately for Max, I was getting the hang of this baby-bathing thing. This enormous love I felt had to be God-given. How else could mothers gush so when the only thing their infant can do is perform public — and generally airborne — bodily functions? But after several months I was beginning to realize that mothering also requires God-given stamina.

I tried to keep up with my freelance design work, but caring for Max was just too intense. My brain felt like its electrical cord had dropped in the water. I was being conditioned to respond to Max's cries and was always wearing this puddle of puke on my shoulder. I went from being this cool, well-dressed graphic designer who actually showered daily to someone who looked like she'd been on an Oklahoma dairy farm in a tornado.

Our slick gray and white home, adorned with expensive original art, became a collage of plastic and quilted fabric and smelled like disinfectant. But it was okay. Actually, it was wonderful. We loved to hold Max, look at him, drink him in like a sweet elixir. Garry and I would dance with Max, swaying with our slumpy little Jell-O-boy, as we listened to pop rock and country-western. Randy Travis and Patsy Cline crooned their melancholy tunes, while we swayed with Max for hours, right through his tears. I'm sure I sang "Walkin' after

Midnight," a bittersweet Patsy Cline song about searching for the one you love, a thousand times while we gazed at our beautiful baby. Max was always looking up, drawn to the skylights in our home. His eyes would widen as the lacey blue of his irises would overtake his pupils. "Skylight," we would whisper in his ear, and he would wave his arms and legs like it was aerobics class.

For the first time in my life I knew exactly what would happen next: I would have more children. I'd be a wife and mother. Other things might change, but not this. I love a guarantee.

The doctor said it was colic. We tried everything to stop the crying. We borrowed a baby swing. Nothing. I tried changing my diet. Nothing. In desperation we even took a friend's advice and turned Max upside down after nursing. Let me spare you the graphic details of freshly swallowed milk combined with gravity. If Max was awake, he was crying, and he was awake all but a few hours a day. Only one thing would calm him: the Snuggly, one of those strap-on-your-front packs for carrying a baby. Max would scrunch down inside where it was dark and quiet, and I would sway back and forth, sometimes for hours, until he finally fell asleep. Then, I would carefully lie down as if I had an explosive device strapped to my chest and steal what sleep I could.

I brought Max to the doctors often. "Why is he crying all the time?" I would ask. "Why is he throwing up all the time?" "Why doesn't he sleep?" At four months something was really bothering me. Max wasn't making eye contact. Actually, he avoided eye contact. The doctor's office said to "wait and see." I wondered if there was a problem with his eyesight. So one day before feeding him, when I made sure I was alone with Max, I put on heavy black eye makeup and bright red lipstick. I looked like a circus clown. He still refused to look at me. As baffled as Max must have been by his freak-show mother, I was even more unsettled. I felt so foolish, catching a glimpse of my desperation as I stood at the mirror to wash my face.

The physical demands of mothering became extraordinary. Friends had cautioned me that caring for a baby would be harder than I could imagine, so I assumed that other new mothers were doing the same hardest-job-they'd-ever-had too. It was only after I asked how the other mothers were existing on two hours of sleep a night, or calmed their children when they cried every waking hour, or how they handled the constant digestive battles, that I caught on. The other mothers in our "Mom and Me" exercise class exchanged glances as if I was suddenly speaking another language. Silence came over the room until finally, someone spoke up. "My baby sleeps all the time," she said. Then another woman joined in: "My baby only cries now when he's hungry." One by one the other mothers shared their stories. I suddenly felt terribly alone in this crowded room, everyone staring at me and my beautiful baby boy.

In the months that followed, I felt increasingly alone. At a weekly playgroup I watched other babies babble while Max only cried. Several began to crawl, while Max struggled to sit. Within a few months the other children were walking and talking and playing together. I would watch from the sidelines, a wallflower, as the other mothers talked and their babies played. All I could do was hold Max in my arms as he helplessly cried for the entire two hours. It was as if he were in pain, burying his face in my neck and gripping at my tear-soaked shoulder. I was back in junior high, desperately wanting to fit in, to be in the cool clique. Everyone tried to assist with ideas to help Max calm down and sit with the other children, but nothing worked.

By the end of the playgroup, with Max finally calm in his car seat, tears would flow silently down my cheeks. I never let anyone see these tears, not even my husband. I couldn't bear that the most perfect time in my life was laced with even a hint of despair. I just kept slipcovering my heart with love for Max so that no one would notice.

I dreaded reading those childcare and development books I'd been addicted to. Max just wasn't hitting the milestones, and yet no one had an answer. Finally, at twelve months old, Max began to crawl. He became happier, healthier, more engaged. He giggled and smiled, the commander of his own carpeted universe. But just a few weeks later, at thirteen months, Max ran a high fever, and a red rash covered his body. Our pediatrician rushed us to the hospital, where they confirmed a diagnosis of a rare disease called Kawasaki syndrome. Thankfully the pediatrician had acted swiftly, and there was no long-term damage to Max's heart as can happen to many children who contract it.

Yet even after treatment, when the doctor expected him to be healthy, Max continued to be sick. Four months passed, and he was still plagued with a persistent fever and flu-like symptoms. It was as if his body just couldn't fight back. One day I was sitting in front of Max's highchair feeding him breakfast after another sleepless night, and the next thing I knew my forehead landed with a thud on his food tray. I sat up, startled, with Cheerio's stuck to my face.

The only thing I knew is that we had to hold on and keep getting back up. Things had to get easier. After all, this was our precious baby. Just a short time ago, before Max existed, I felt whole and complete. Now, if you removed this love from my being, there would be nothing left of me but a vapor. I had become my love for Max, our luminous little skylight boy. We would get through this. It's what families do.

CHAPTER 6

WALKING

Over the next few months Max's behavior didn't change, but my husband's did. Garry called one day to tell me he really needed us to go out together that night. "Tonight? I don't think it's a good idea tonight," I responded, naively. Max was sick with a fever and wouldn't stop crying. It was exhausting caring for him while he was still so ill after his Kawasaki syndrome. I should have welcomed the break. But I'd grown up in the 1960s and flashed back to all those news stories of babysitters taking acid and cooking babies in the oven like turkeys. Garry couldn't figure out why I didn't want to get away, and I couldn't figure out why he didn't want to get closer. We didn't go out.

But I thought it was okay. I thought I was supposed to help Max when he was so desperately needy. Actually, I just did it without thinking. But somewhere in the process, I hadn't noticed my husband's needs. I felt a little crazy, unable to understand why my job as mom was so much harder than it was for other mothers. Garry couldn't understand it either.

Where was my rodeo cowboy, the man who was so incredibly confident when Max was born? Certainly our lives had turned upside down, but that's part of having children, isn't it? I'd left my job, my social life, my basic ability to bathe like other human beings, and I felt vulnerable. I was more dependent on my husband than ever. I was like one of those little dogs that look so muscular and confident until they get wet and their fur mats down revealing all their pinkness and frailty. But I thought it was safe. I thought my husband understood it was only wet hair.

Garry became suddenly distant, almost silent, for several weeks. As much as I longed for Max to say his first word, I was tortured that now my husband was refusing to speak, refusing to let me into his thoughts. His silence made me feel desperate. We had always dealt with adversity differently. I would throw myself on a problem like it was a live hand grenade, while Garry would fold his arms and look away with absolute certainty that the pin had never actually come out. Reality usually divided us by falling somewhere in the middle. I hoped that the upcoming trip we planned to Florida might give us some much-needed time together. But at the last minute, my husband announced that he couldn't leave work and insisted that I take Max and visit my family without him. I was crushed and a little sick to my stomach, as if there was a secret everyone knew but me. When we returned home, life was anything but right.

I sat in the family room on the edge of our overstuffed gray couch and waited for my husband to sit beside me. I nervously curled a sheet of paper in my hand, a list I'd written in Florida of all the things I thought I could do to make things better. But Garry took a seat some distance away and refused to look me in the eyes. I could feel every muscle tense as I waited for him to speak after so much silence.

I didn't see it coming. I hadn't heard his subtle call for help. Or maybe I'd just turned my attention to the one whose cries were loudest. When he finally spoke, he kept his head down, his gaze fixed on the floor, as words fell from his mouth like molten lava dividing our lives. I kept staring at him; he looked the same. He looked exactly like my husband. But he wasn't. I wrapped my arms around myself and leaned into my knees, certain that pain and anger would cause my body to break apart. A thousand thoughts beat against me like pounding fists.

I struggled to keep my focus. I looked past my husband's shoulder, his eyes never lifting to meet mine, and forced myself to look for

Max. Where was he? I had completely lost track of him, of how long it had even been since I saw him last. When I found Max my eyes rested on him as if he were the last sign of life on the planet, the last shred of beauty. Just eighteen months old, he was snuggled into a soft, blue one-piece suit. Max had been avoiding us, perfectly quiet. Although he rarely seemed connected to his surroundings he must have sensed the heartbreak that existed in the room. Just one week earlier Max had taken his long-awaited first steps. He was walking. Now he had found his way across the room and was steadying himself on the sill of a window. Sunlight streamed through the glass, bathing him in translucent light. His blond hair floated above his head, and his skin glowed as if the light was within him.

That night I brought Max up to his room but couldn't bear to put him in his crib. I sat in our Kennedy rocker with my arms, my body, my soul wrapped around him, and rocked. The house felt so empty, even in his nursery filled with soft stuffed animals and happy, colorful wallpaper. My mouth was dry, and I struggled to breathe past the lump that sat in my throat like a wad of shredded wool. I prayed, with tears of desperation, rigid with anger. "Do something, Lord," I pleaded. "Do something, please."

I felt a cool rush of hope. I won't allow this to happen, I thought. I'll refuse to give up. "I promise, Max," I breathed as I watched over him. "I'm going to give you Mom and Dad together. You are going to have your family." I didn't know it then, but it was a promise I couldn't keep. Over time, I would have to learn to walk forward, alone, with Max.

I HADN'T EATEN IN SEVERAL DAYS but felt as though I weighed a thousand pounds. Heather's kitchen was white and spotless and filled with the sweet smell of blueberry cake. It was her turn to host the playgroup, and I just had to get out of the house, even for something

Max might cry through. Max wiggled from my arms and stood on the linoleum floor, a very brave thing indeed.

"And how is Max today?" Heather asked in her British accent as she leaned into him.

"He took his first steps," I responded as I set him down to try. All the other toddlers had learned to walk months ago. Ironically, this was Max's moment to shine. He wobbled on his little white shoes, all scuffed at the toes from crawling, and then turned back to me in a moment of sheer panic. I pulled him into my arms.

Heather looked closely at my face, perfectly made-up to hide my swollen eyes. I had to say it, to release the truth before it shattered me. "Garry left four days ago. He walked out. I don't know where he is." The women rushed around me as if I'd been sprayed with shards of glass. I didn't want these women to see my pain, these mothers who were doing everything right, who had husbands that stayed with them. But I didn't have the strength to hide. I let these women with their seemingly perfect lives see my frailty, all my wet hair. And in return, they fed me warm blueberry cake and comforted me like a young child.

That afternoon I took Max to the beach — anything to avoid our empty house. We were both so small on that endless stretch of water and sky. Max didn't like to touch the sand but was happy in my lap as long as I sang. I needed him in my arms as much as he needed me. I began to sing "Walkin' after Midnight," that same melancholy country-western song about searching for love, searching for happiness. Max loved this song. The air was filled with the muffled sounds of gulls and crashing waves. Children were running up and down the beach, in and out of the ocean, with mothers and fathers watching. And I felt we weren't whole anymore.

I pressed my feet into the warm sand and buried my face in my precious toddler. Had any of this been real, or had it all been a lie? Struggling to breathe I slipped into prayer as if it were an oxygen mask, each breath unable to exist without longing for God to lift us from this, to protect us, to provide.

CHAPTER 7

FALLING DOWN
THE STAIRS

If I could have disengaged myself from the situation, perhaps I would have understood why my husband had the impulse to flee. But fleeing turned into months of court appearances, bitter disagreements, and soaring legal fees. I couldn't get my bearings.

Cathy, a woman I'd met at church and barely knew, hired a babysitter one day and came with me into court so that I wouldn't be alone. She didn't know anything about divorce law, but I felt bigger with her beside me. The courthouse hallways were filled with clumps of assorted angry individuals straggling around waiting for their shot at justice. Cathy and I looked like we'd stopped at a biker bar to ask directions to the nearest Ann Taylor store. We found a beaten-up wooden bench in the back corner of the building where we could wait until I was called into court. Its seat was covered with carved initials that caught my stockings on the splintered wood, and the rusted radiator beside us hissed and banged at me as I tried to pray.

On our final day in court, eighteen months after it all began, the voices of dark-suited lawyers echoed against the cavernous walls. I couldn't move. My feet felt bolted to the ground while parts of my life were sucked out of my reach, gone forever, as if someone opened the door of an airplane midflight. I looked across the room, past the judge, to see Garry, still my husband, whispering to his lawyer, nodding, writing notes. He looked different now that he didn't love me. Maybe it was my eyes that had changed.

I didn't think I could hate so deeply as the day Max and I had to move from our home. I was out in the driveway shoveling snow before the moving truck came. It was snowing so hard that it was even coming up from the ground. I was pouring sweat under my heavy down coat, seething with anger at my now ex-husband for leaving us in a house I couldn't afford, for leaving me alone, for making it snow so hard that day. I swung the shovel hurling heavy snow over my shoulder, furious that I had ever let myself become so vulnerable.

After the moving van pulled away, I went back to the house. It was empty, every sign of our lives there gone. Just clean, I told myself. Don't get caught up in the memories. People were telling me to "move on" and "get on with your life." One well-meaning friend even told me to set a date and only let myself hurt until then. If that could work, I'd set a date to wake up six inches taller and with better eyesight. I knew they meant well. They just wanted me to be okay, immediately. I was trying my hardest, but life wasn't okay.

I couldn't wait to get out of that shell of a house, but I was the cleaning crew before the new owners came in. I scrubbed that place with the energy of a trapped squirrel, scurrying up and down the stairs, running on my little wheel so that I wouldn't feel. Now, I know how to vacuum stairs — you stand below the vacuum and clean the step above rather than leaning down over the appliance like a hunchback. But I wasn't thinking. In my mind-numbing frenzy I leaned a little too far over the vacuum and suddenly found myself flying over the handle like a pole-vaulter. I got some good air before I sideswiped the wall and crashed against the floor six steps below. The vacuum landed just next to me with its engine whining and brushes spinning. I sat on the carpet stunned, my pulse thumping in my temples, amazed that I hadn't been injured. My heart was another story.

Max and I were little birds fallen from a nest, lying on the grass with badly broken wings. I wanted God to pick us up, set us back on a branch, place us safely in another nest. I wanted God to restore us to the same shiny life we once had. Be patient, God must have thought, there *is* a plan.

AS ALONE AS I FELT, there were people who loved us. At the time, only my mom lived within driving distance while the rest of my family lived in different parts of the country. But even at a distance they were all with us, helping in every way they could. As packed as my dad's schedule can be, we spoke every day, sometimes several times a day. You would have thought he had nothing else important to do. I would hear his voice and hold the phone as if I were clinging to my dad's hand. And my mom would show up to help with Max, and bring us food. One day she even showed up with a small starter trampoline. We set it up in the middle of our living room, of course.

And our little church, unconventional and nondenominational, with its stark warehouse setting, spoon fed us tiny mouthfuls of love and warmth. Max loved to come to church with me, bouncing on my lap during the music and running wild during coffee hour. A friend used to call Max "the Babe," saying that he ran like Babe Ruth, all determination with little gracefulness. One day, the church gave each of the single mothers a check when it had "extra money." I needed the help more than I would have admitted. And it was at this church where we met Patti and her husband, Nick. The first time I arrived at church, suddenly alone with Max, they scooped us up as if we were family and brought us into their lovely home. "You must do a lot of traveling," I said as I looked around their living room. "You have such ... unusual pieces of art." Patti threw her head back with a laugh that sounded like music. "Nick has an eye for treasure," she said with poise. "He's rescued all these things from the town dump."

The church showed up to help Max and me move into a rental house. But I never fully unpacked. I left most of our lives in boxes stacked in the basement. And every other weekend I had to hand my precious towheaded toddler over to his father for the night. I would hold Max in my arms until the very last second, until he slipped from my fingers, taking my last breath of life with him. Where did they go? What did they do? Max couldn't tell me. Garry was already remarried and lived on the other side of our small New England town a million miles away.

CHAPTER 8

GRACE

With some extraordinary help from family, Max and I bought "the Frog Pond House," a small house on a quiet street, which we named after the three-foot-wide goldfish pond in the backyard — which Max fell into on our first visit. It was a baptism of sorts into our new lives together, except that my little toddler looked like the Swamp Thing. I filled the pond in immediately. The house was perfect for the two of us, and the ocean was at the end of the street, just a few houses away. The breeze was salty and a foghorn assured us with its slow, distant call.

On our first night there I didn't want Max to be afraid. I was tired of being afraid too. So I brought him into my room and the two of us held hands and jumped on my big bed for hours. We floated on my white down comforter until we had filled every inch of that house with love and laughter, forcing out every intruding doubt. We were like animals marking our territory. And then I tucked Max in right next to me, wrapping my sweet two-year-old in a billowing cloud of softness. We had survived. We were home.

I spent the next months ripping off wallpaper and plastering my own walls as some odd sort of therapy, the only goal to make something smooth and even, so unlike the rest of my life. I could lose myself in those walls, spackle over the pain. But no matter how hard I tried, it kept coming back to the surface.

As Christmas approached I was overjoyed that my dad and Patty sent us tickets to visit them in Florida. I packed so much stuff that by the time we arrived I felt as if we'd hiked through the Himalayas. I had a car seat over one arm, Max in his stroller in the other, and a huge pack of toys and books and bribes strapped to my back. Fortunately, the weather in Florida meant we didn't need to pack many clothes, otherwise we would have needed a crowd of Sherpas. But a week with my dad and Patty would be a time of refuge, a place to let everything wash away in the gentle Gulf.

I remember this visit especially. I had been feeling so isolated, so starved for love and support that even a simple conversation was a thrill. So when close friends of my parents came to visit, along with their son and his fiancé, it was a party. Patty had made hors d'oeuvre's, and I felt as though I'd landed back on my feet for a moment, sipping seltzer out of a real glass goblet, talking to real people as we mingled in the living room. I wrapped myself in this snapshot of normal like a warm robe, even though it was trimmed with denial. Max was fine for the first five minutes, playing on the floor and jumping in my lap.

And then he wasn't.

Max couldn't cope with people unless they were on the floor playing trains with him. These were dignified people who weren't there to crawl around the carpet with a two-year-old. I didn't think anyone noticed when I took Max to the backroom and stayed there with him for the next hour and a half, alone. I could hear their voices mumbling in the background, punctuated with bursts of laughter. I kept thinking how beautiful and perfect these people looked. They were slick and coiffed, the way I looked as a designer. Actually, the fact that they had showered put them in a different social class. I was Pigpen, the little comic strip character, walking along with an enormous cloud of soil billowing around me. I read books to Max, and we played with blocks, something I normally loved, but it felt hollow. Wasn't anyone missing us? I felt I'd been assigned to the wobbly little aluminum children's table in the kitchen, while all the fancy guests enjoyed the real party. Aching with loneliness, I could hear them starting to say their good-byes. But before they left I overheard the man say, "Emily is so filled with grace. You can just see it in her."

Grace? Was that my consolation prize? If this man could see grace, how did he miss seeing my enormous swirling turmoil? It made me furious — and jealous of their seemingly perfect lives. I didn't need velvet-covered clichés. I needed love and comfort. I needed help.

It was the week before Christmas, a time when my dad and Patty always delivered their ministry's Angel Tree gifts to local families whose children have a parent in prison. Max and I went along for the ride even though Max might be too afraid to enter the home and be a part of the delivery. I could always take him outside or wait in the car.

On the way there, Max sat in his car seat, sucking on his fingers, as the forty-minute drive lulled him. We talked about the family we were going to visit, the names and ages of the two little girls, and of the grandmother who was caring for them. Max just stared out the window as we drove along, and as I now know, was cataloging every street sign so that he could recite them back to me some ten years later. Dad and Patty and I tried to simplify the concept, bring it down to the basics, hoping that Max might soak in something of the experience. "These children don't have their mom or dad with them right now," I said, "so they might feel a little sad. They need some love." Max didn't have any language to respond and, at that point, never responded positively to anything except being in my arms, my singing, the pool, or his books and trains. He never even turned when someone called his name. Max just stared out the window as I braced myself for the next challenge. The smoothly paved highway turned onto a rocky dirt road as we approached a clearing in the thick tropical foliage.

The dried beige lawn was newly mown around the tiny yellow ranch house the size of a trailer. The grandmother was standing on a wooden deck waiting for us, waving us in, watching as we stepped out of the car. I scooped Max into my arms and, with trepidation, followed my dad through the sliding glass door. A plate of cookies sat on the cloth-draped table surrounded by well-worn teacups, typically a lovely symbol of hospitality. But I couldn't imagine Max and me lingering over a cup of tea. I searched across the room to find the two young girls, just a little older than Max, both with white blonde hair in a pageboy cut. The youngest one was kneeling on the blue shag carpet playing with a toy. The other little girl was engulfed in an overpadded maroon recliner, sitting with her legs straight out, her feet never reaching the edge of the seat. She was smiling at us with a giggle that desperately wanted to escape.

I held Max in my arms, bouncing him a bit on my hip to reassure him of my presence in this new environment, trying to stave off the inevitable tears. But he began to kick his feet and wiggle his torso as if he were trying to evade my grasp. As I set him down he rushed over to the little girl in the chair, tottering on his wobbly legs, until he reached her side. He leaned into her, pushing his face against her, and rested there a moment. Then he turned around and walked toward the other little girl on the floor. Max bent over and pressed his cheek against her cheek until their blonde hair and pink faces melted into one. They didn't move. Everything stopped. When time began again, Max turned and walked right back to me. I lifted him into my arms and looked at my dad, who was staring at me, wide-eyed. He was trying not to exclude this gracious grandmother as he spoke to me. "Did you see that, Emily? Did you see that?" He turned to the grand-mother, trying to explain that this was not Max's normal behavior, but his words fell short. Something had washed over Max, a wave of inexplicable, unexpected beauty enabling him to express love beyond our understanding. This child who was incapable of uttering a single word, spoke more clearly that day than any of us.

WHEN WE RETURNED HOME to Massachusetts after our Florida vaca-tion, I was determined to find the help we needed. But I had to get past the barriers of insurance companies, medical bureaucracy, and waiting lists before we could see the specialists who might give me an answer to Max's language and developmental delays. Weeks and months went by. It was an arduous process. I discovered that doors don't just open; you have to keep knocking, pushing, sometimes wedging your foot in the door. And you don't even know where to begin.

At age three, Max certainly wasn't growing out of any of the problems. He wasn't even speaking except for a few partial words like "mah" for mom and "ju" for juice. And there was this one hallucinogenic moment, when Max stood up and recited one of his books from start to finish, and then sat back down unable to speak. And his interests were odd. Everywhere he went he carried a purple plastic donut and the lid from a jar of peanut butter. If a shoe fell off he would cry as if he had lost a foot. His energy level was unlike any hypercaffeinated state I had ever achieved. On our first visit to his special-needs preschool Max careened around the room pulling out every drawer and dumping the contents on the floor. The teacher looked at me with her eyes bugging out, probably wondering how I managed to actually get dressed that morning, and said, "Oh, my. You must be a little busy."

I'D BEEN WAITING FOR NEARLY a year for an appointment with the doctors at a Boston hospital, and now that the time had arrived, I hated to go. No one ever wants their four-year-old child evaluated by a team of developmental specialists, but I needed answers. We left our house at 6:00 a.m. and fought our way through the commuter traffic. The drive alone tested me, but then we met up with my ex-husband and his new wife. Well, "met up" wouldn't exactly be the term. We never even spoke.

Max and I were placed in a room with a one-way mirror allowing several of the specialists to observe at a distance while each evaluator had a turn to test Max. Garry sat behind that glass too, conducting his own evaluation. I felt so self-conscious, as if someone stuck a "kick me" sign on my back that I couldn't reach. And the testing wasn't going well. "Max, what is this?" they would ask, pointing to a block. Max would look away, jumping in and out of his seat. We'd already been through auditory testing and his hearing was fine. "Max, look at this," they commanded, chasing him with their eyes as he crawled underneath the table. I knew he didn't have the words, but he clearly didn't understand or even have the ability to pay attention. I wanted desperately to jump in and redirect Max, to be the translator, but I had to remain silent. The specialists scribbled secret hieroglyphics on their notepads and tried to hide them from my view. I searched their faces, thirsting for a clue. And I felt as though my ex-husband's eyes were boring a hole into the back of my neck.

After several hours of testing, and a closed-door session for the evaluators only, they brought Max and me into a brightly colored playroom to talk. Garry and his wife had already left. This room was much larger, and the mirrors on the wall actually appeared to be mirrors — I didn't think anyone was watching us, but I wasn't sure. I took a seat on the edge of a vinyl-covered hassock, and Max started playing on a little slide beside me. I'd waited months for the opportunity to talk with these experts. I could almost hear the cavalry's trumpets blaring in the distance. They asked me questions, but they were no longer scribbling notes on their pads. Their demeanor became disturbingly calm, their monotone voices like a dull train roar you hear in the distance before a tornado hits. I sat alone facing these four specialists who were lined up in child-sized chairs like a low-lying firing squad armed with a freshly inked "Secret" stamped across their papers. They wouldn't tell me that day, but they all knew then that it was autism.

I hung on to every question, trying to answer as best as I could, but I was exhausted. Max was tired too and was trying to climb into my lap, distracting me. I reached down to lift him as I continued talking, looking past him so that I wouldn't waste a minute of this precious time. But Max persisted, throwing himself into a huge belly-flopped hug, like Garfield on the inside of a car window. He pressed his cheek, soft as a rose petal, against mine. I fought it for a moment and then, uncontrollably, lowered my face into his, closed my eyes as if he had drugged me, and melted into him. The room disappeared. The specialists disappeared, their voices fading into a mist. All the judgments on my beloved child washed away in my arms. I wasn't going to waste a minute of this precious time. Indeed, this is *grace*, the help I needed, the gift I can't survive without: a beautiful, unexpected, inexplicably perfect love raining down upon us even in the midst of the darkest moments.

"What a big day you've had, Maxi," I whispered into his ear. "You did a great job." I could hear *oohs* and *ahs* from the four evaluators, as if love and grace lapped over the sides, spilling onto them and soaking all their notes.

CHAPTER 9

LOCKED IN A CLOSET

I was relieved, actually, to finally have a diagnosis. Little did I know then that labeling Max "autistic" would place me smack in the center of a war zone. For the next three years I would find myself fighting to get the services Max needed, forcing my foot in the door of every specialist. I became a self-confessed autism-conference-junkie, a Dead Head following the different specialists wherever they were speaking. I read everything I could get my hands on, sat up at night studying medical journals written with words that aren't even in the dictionary. And I would cart around my notepad of strategies like Moses carrying the Ten Commandments.

During that time Max was in a specialized school program for autistic children and received therapy almost every afternoon. I can't say that it was going well, that my now-seven-year-old was even making much progress, but optimism is survival. And having a team of professionals working with Max should have been empowering. We all sat around a table together one afternoon, the classroom supervisor along with Max's teachers and therapists, to plan his education for the upcoming year. Finally, Max was going to have a chance to be included in a regular-education classroom in his public school. I leaned forward and locked eyes with everyone at the table.

"Let's set the goals high," I said excitedly. "Push for progress. I think we're going to see great things from Max this year."

The supervisor interrupted me, grabbing the spotlight. "Well …," he responded with a dull note of sarcasm, "you know Max is ... *extremely* disabled." I watched closely as he lowered his face and opened his eyes widely as if surprised. "He's *severely* autistic ... I mean ... in all my years I've *never* seen a child *quite ... so ...*," and then he left the sentence hanging with nothing but a smirk on his face.

I bristled so hard that cactus spines popped out of my shoulders. "Max is going to be a bridge designer someday," I spat back at him. "He knows everything about bridges, about architecture." Every day Max would study books with photographs of bridges and memorize hundreds of names and facts. I'd watch him create intricate bridge replicas out of Legos or blocks or silverware or anything he could get his hands on. They were exquisite and unexpected, a glimmer of brilliance. I pictured Max someday learning architectural computer programs and designing beautiful structures. "Max is going to design bridges someday," I insisted. I poked my finger toward the supervisor, "You just watch." The room fell silent.

I was beginning to resemble one of those cartoon characters that gets run over by a truck, flat as a pancake, and then stands back up with tire tracks printed across their shirt. And then the next sound you hear is the horn blast of another truck. But tonight I was too excited to get out of the road, to turn out my light and go to sleep. Tomorrow would be the conference I'd been waiting months to attend. The keynote speaker was known for his ability to improve the behavior of children with autism, help them understand and follow directions, even stop their tantrums. But what truly enticed me was the murmur that some of the children he had worked with improved so significantly that they actually lost their diagnosis of autism.

The next morning at 5:30, I slammed my hand against the alarm. I shouldn't have stayed up so late again. I didn't have to wake Max, who was with his dad. I rushed through my shower, grabbed a few granola bars, and drove for two hours.

I arrived early enough to stake out a great seat at the conference, up close and dead center. The auditorium was packed with teachers and parents, searching for clues, desperate for hope. Specialists in the field of autism didn't have all the answers, but maybe they knew more than we did. They had power. As we listened to them speak, their words rang with the sound of jingling keys in the pocket of a prison guard, each of us hoping they might unlock our child's world.

Another caffeine-infused parent sat beside me, taking notes just as fast as I was. "Do you know about the 'window'?" she whispered, as she leaned over the notebook propped on her lap. I nodded my head and smiled, trying not to engage in conversation. I didn't want to miss a word of the presentation. Of course I knew — we all knew — wondering if it was still open for our children.

The "window" was the only thing the autism specialists agreed upon: those first few years of life when the brain is malleable and treatment for autism is most effective, even, as they would tell us, curable. But it wasn't that simple. It was the mid-1990s, and autism was not as prevalent as it is today. Most of our children were not diagnosed until the window of time had almost closed. And to make matters more complicated, there wasn't an agreed-upon formula for treatment. Parents who stood within this closing window were forced to guess which path of treatment might be right for their child.

There was an endless list of treatment options: vitamins, play therapy, applied behavioral analysis, diets, medications, auditory training, occupational therapy, speech therapy, and more. Some even recommended swimming with dolphins. And each school of treatment had an almost militant following. Even getting your child into a treatment program was a battle. Those with young children tried everything possible to pull their kid through the window. Those of us with older children, who feared the window would soon close, wondered how we could have possibly done more. The window became our greatest hope — and our constant heartache.

But this day, at this conference, there was hope. I grabbed on to every word of the presentation by the doctor I had waited so anxiously to hear from, knowing it could be the right treatment for Max. At the end of this daylong conference, with palms sweating, I stood in line to speak with him. I straightened my posture and tried to appear confident as if applying for a job.

When it was my turn I asked, "How can I create this kind of program for my son?"

The doctor's chest puffed up like a salesman who just saw his customer reach for her purse and asked, "How old is your son?"

"Seven," I replied with a strong voice to match his.

He barely gave me another look as he turned to the next parent in line, mumbling, "Oh, he's too old. It's too late. This won't work."

I pleaded for his attention, for another chance at hope, but he dismissed me as if I were begging on the street.

THAT NIGHT I LAY IN BED AND CURLED the pillow around my head, trying to muffle the sound of his words. Apparently, the window of healing had slammed shut. But how could Max possibly be over the hill at age seven? He still had a smile full of baby teeth with square holes where someday the real ones would arrive. His little hands were puffy and undefined, like dough rising under his buttery skin. He even sported his first pair of big-boy underpants, proudly snapping the elastic waist against his perfectly round belly.

I knew I was doing everything I could to help Max. He'd started speech and educational therapy at age two; occupational and physical therapy followed soon after. He'd been in a specialized school program since age three. We'd tried traditional and alternative interventions, some too bizarre to admit. I'd even worked with a doctor and tried medication as a means to soothe my seven-year-old's anxiety. That was several months ago, at the start of summer vacation, and an experience I'll never forget.

As always, Max had been waking at night, but with this trial of medication he suddenly became agitated, destructive, even aggressive, knocking over lamps and running at me full speed. I couldn't get upset or it would make matters worse; Max couldn't understand the cause and effect of emotions, of why I might be angry or sad or scared. When morning would come, Max didn't appear to even remember what he'd done, although communication between us was cryptic at best.

One fateful night, after a month of being sleep deprived and desperate, I made what I believed to be an unusually responsible parenting decision. Rather than climbing into the bell tower and shooting at the neighborhood, I yanked the blanket and pillow from my bed and walked down the stairs. As I lay on the couch, pounding my fists into the blanket as if I were staking a tent, I noticed it was very quiet upstairs. Too quiet. As much as I deserved sleep *at all costs*, I took a deep breath and went back up. All I could see was a lump bulging under Max's puffy white comforter. I peeled back the top corner and found my son balled up and shaking, staring up at me wild-eyed. I called the doctor the next day and told him to either take Max off the medication or prescribe some for me too. Thankfully, after several days drug-free, Max was back to himself.

Even with all these attempts and interventions, I had a dull ache in my gut, like hunger or the way you feel when you stand too close to the edge of a balcony. Had I missed something? Did I choose the wrong school, the wrong therapy? Max had made progress, but it was agonizingly slow.

I couldn't let go of this presenter's words and his dismissal of my child as hopeless. I was desperate for Max to be one of those kids who loses his diagnosis of autism and just ends up with some regular childhood trauma like ears that are too big or pimples. I was persistent, calling this presenter, this leading expert in autism, until his office finally gave me an appointment in his "so-busy-we-can't-possibly-fit-you-in" schedule. There is a looser criterion for "stalking" when it comes to parents calling these doctors. I'm not sure if I really believed in his ideas, or if I just couldn't stand that he didn't believe in Max.

By the time the doctor arrived at our home for the appointment, several months later, Max had actually turned eight, but I wasn't about to point that out. We exchanged introductions and I offered him coffee, tea, water. I was ready to give him my car if he'd help us. We sat together at my dining room table so that I could spread out my dutifully organized notes and questions. I had copies of the visuals that Max used to help him learn and, as Max was still at school, a few photographs to make it more personal. If he could just see a picture of Max, witness firsthand his youthful promise, he would have to help.

I began to explain some of our challenges — tantrums, anxiety, communication, sleeplessness. And of course I threw in a few endearing anecdotes, just to let him catch my enthusiasm. He listened quietly, leaning one elbow on the table, but was all business. After a few minutes he reached into his briefcase for his yellow pad and pen. He then reeled off a list of questions.

"And how often do these tantrums occur?" he asked as he hunched over his paper.

"Well, it depends on the demands," I answered.

He was poised with his pen but wasn't yet writing.

"Once a week I guess, maybe less," I said.

"And the duration?" He was still looking down at his blank page.

"Oh, they can last a long time. Sometimes an hour," I said. "I think it's hard for him to calm down once he's upset."

He wrote much more than I thought I said. It was quiet for a little too long, so I anxiously blurted out more. "As I said before, it's anxiety. He's scared of everything. The toughest thing is when we're out somewhere, like a store. If he starts to melt down it's really hard to get him out. I can't just pick him up anymore." I rolled my eyes and gave a half smile. "That's where we need help."

"Hmm," he breathed as he continued scratching notes.

"Can you teach these kids to walk through a grocery store without a tantrum?" I pressed, searching for a little off-the-cuff conversation, a little hope.

"Let's get through some basics first," he said, peering up at me over his reading glasses. "Is he noncompliant at home?"

"Well, how do you define that?" I asked, feeling reprimanded.

"Does he refuse to do something when you ask?" he said, looking intensely into my eyes. I couldn't tell whether he was totally engrossed in the topic, or secretly irritated that I had badgered him into helping me.

I thought about it for a moment. "Yes," I answered.

He wrote another long answer.

"But he has a processing delay," I explained, using my hands for emphasis. "Sometimes he just needs time to understand what I said to him. I usually give him ten seconds to process, and then ask him again. And sometimes he does it after — "

"So he's noncompliant," he interrupted, still looking down, still writing.

"Well ... yes. But — "

"And how often is he noncompliant?"

This was not the energetic presenter I had seen at the conference. He was reserved, clinical. His voice and expression never changed from one question to the next, for the entire two hours we sat at that table. I thought he might offer suggestions and ideas.

"I'd like to take a look around the house, if I may," he said, arching his back in a stretch and setting his pen down across his papers.

"Sure," I said as I jumped up, so happy to move from the table, to be released from the interrogation. I smoothed out the creases in my pants from sitting in one position for so long, hoping my sweat wasn't showing through, and took him on a tour. "As long as you forgive the mess in my studio." I smiled. Actually, I had just cleaned it in case he glanced in there, but I thought that line might win some points.

He did much more than glance. He looked in every room. He even opened every closet and studied the contents. He wasn't saying a word. "Are you … looking for something?" I asked politely, following at the brisk heel of his khaki pants like a puppy dog.

He didn't even turn to look at me. "Ahh … yes," he breathed, as he continued to search.

He reminded me of one of those guys in high school who thought he was too cool to acknowledge your existence, even if you tripped over his foot.

Maybe he actually *was* analyzing my housekeeping skills. How is that linked to autism? Maybe he thought he was going to find something incriminating, some evidence that I was a bad mother, like a bottle of scotch with a sippy-cup lid.

He finally made his way to the front hall and stood for a minute with the coat closet door wide open. "Is there a light somewhere?" he asked.

"Oh, just for the hall. It's right here," I said, jumping behind him to flip the switch. He was so tall in our little house with low ceilings that his head eclipsed the recessed light above him, casting his huge shadow into the closet. He just stood there for a minute, with his hand still resting on the doorknob, and stared into the dark and cluttered space.

"You'll have to empty this," he said, still studying the contents.

I was lost.

"And put a lock on the outside," he continued. "You could do that yourself."

I stared up at his towering frame, waiting for an explanation.

"When Max is noncompliant … as soon as he refuses to comply with a request," he advised, now in the same strong voice he used presenting at the conference, "you should immediately lock him into this closet."

There was silence. I waited for him to laugh, smile, anything. I could feel my forehead wrinkle and my eyes squint, as if the light were suddenly too bright. I turned my eyes away from him for a moment and looked into the tiny cramped closet just to be sure that it was actually, indeed, still a closet.

He offered me a few sentences about his theory, but I couldn't hear him anymore. Is this the same man who claims to cure kids with autism? The specialist I hunted down as if I were a crazed groupie? There's not a chance in the world that I'd take his advice. The doctor just shook my limp hand and assured me that I would receive his bill and written report in the mail.

I was horrified at this man, but angrier with myself for running down the wrong path and wasting precious time. It seemed everyone believed the window of healing had closed. Now it appeared that even doors were closing, threatening to lock Max out of life. If they were right, the opportunity to reach and change Max was slipping away. I held on to hope that the window of healing might still be open just enough to let in a crack of light, just enough to let us see the world outside of autism. I just didn't know how much there was to hope for.

CHAPTER 10

CHILDREN'S HOSPITAL WITH PATTI

I hadn't given up on specialists, even after the one who wanted to lock my son in a closet. Max's needs were too great to get discouraged. And autism gurus were cropping up as fast as autism rates were rising. I made an appointment at a well-respected Boston hospital for a "communication and technology evaluation." That's where a team of doctors determines if different computer programs or technological devices would help a child better communicate. And communication could open up Max's world, not hide him behind closed doors.

I knew it would be impossible to manage my eight-year-old through the lengthy registration process, let alone the appointment. So my friend Patti came along to help. Max was comfortable with his "Peppermint Patti," naming her after the Peanuts character that graced the side of his cereal box. To Max it raised Patti up a notch to cartoon stardom.

Patti had been a part of our journey from the first time we met her in church. Max was just a baby then, and Patti immediately welcomed the two of us into her home for brunch and then dinner and then late-night movies. Sometimes Patti cared for Max when I had an appointment. She was there when Max was first diagnosed too, back when he was four. When I got the news I called my family — then I called Patti.

"Do you think the diagnosis is right, Em?" she asked me on the phone back then. "Do you think Max has *autism*?"

I felt so beaten down, as if only the top of my head was peeking out above soil. I hadn't even considered questioning the diagnosis. "I ... guess so," I replied.

And then I remember Patti letting out this little sigh; it was almost musical, like the wind through a screen door. There was a very long pause. When Patti finally spoke her voice became direct and authoritative, as if her words were sinking into wet cement. "It might not seem true now, Emily. But God works through these children. They are a *gift*," she said gently, her voice rising and falling like a melody. "Max is a *gift*."

Sometime later Patti told me she had actually taught children with autism. Just after graduating from Gordon College she had worked at a residential program for autistic teenage boys. There she had seen autism at its best and worst. One day over coffee at her kitchen island, this petite, softly rounded, demure woman told me how she once restrained a two-hundred-pound hormone-infused boy in the grocery store when he got "a bit out of hand," as she put it. With her refined manner and Canadian accent she made it sound as if he simply didn't stir his tea with the proper spoon. But she assured me that Max was different than the boys she taught; Max, she would tell me, was going to be fine.

Thereafter Patti was on speed dial when I needed an understanding friend, my throat often hoarse with emotion, as I told her of my fights and frustration with the school system or the parties Max didn't get invited to or any of our other daily disasters. Patti knew the Bible front to back and was always pulling up a Scripture to encourage me, even when I was really looking for a verse about locusts and plagues descending upon the enemy. Most friends would hear my tales of woe and express their empathy by jumping into the frenzy and stirring up my agitation. But that wasn't Patti. She would listen quietly, pensively, letting out that familiar gentle sigh, telling me she heard my words deep within her soul. And when I was finished, she would say only one thing: "They don't see the gift, Emily. They don't know Max is a gift."

On this day I was so glad to have Patti with us as Max and I arrived at the hospital in Boston for our communication and technology evaluation, especially since the patient registration area looked like the Department of Motor Vehicles. Long lines stretched in front of the counters, and people were lying limp across chairs as if they'd slept the night there waiting for their turn. We finally made it to the waiting room of the communication clinic, wheeling Max in a stroller that should have collapsed under his weight forty pounds ago. As it turned out, that high-priced, dual-exhaust, German-engineered model we purchased when I was expecting Max was a pretty good investment.

A doctor finally called us into the office. I was thankful for Patti's help through the lengthy registration process, but I suddenly felt a little uncomfortable, as if I didn't want anyone else to see Max tested, to see all his weaknesses and vulnerabilities. So with my heavy armor clinking and squeaking, I took Max's hand and told Patti we'd be back. She looked at me as the door closed with a knowing little smile on her face that was much too generous.

Three doctors sat in the room, surrounded by wall-to-wall computers. Machines with flashing buttons were everywhere, high and low, humming and blinking. One doctor asked Max to take a seat in a little chair facing the three of them so that they could "have a talk," probably the most frightening three words you could say to Max. They stared for a minute, quietly studying him. "Hello, Max," one finally said in a very grown-up voice. "I'm Doctor So-and-so." There was a long pause. "How are you?" he asked. There was another long pause. "We're going to do some testing with you today." There was only silence. I aged several years. The three doctors stared.

To engage Max you have to follow the same principles as advertising — reach your target audience within three seconds or you've missed your chance. This was bribe time. I reached into my bag of tricks and pulled out an orange lollipop. Max smiled and grabbed it.

"Ohhh," the doctors all said in unison.

"For everyone," I said in an animated voice, passing lollipops to each of them.

The three doctors grinned and exchanged glances while they held up their treats. I felt like I'd arrived at Oktoberfest where the only common language is beer. They all smiled and followed Max's lead in slowly unwrapping their lollipops. Max tasted his. They tasted theirs. And then a computer beeped.

Max jumped out of his seat and frantically started to push the button on the computer.

"No, no," one of the doctors reprimanded.

I pictured myself receiving a bill for two hundred thousand dollars in equipment damages, so I sprung to my feet and tried to put my hand over the button on the computer. Apparently, that is the international symbolic gesture for *please push every other button you can reach*. I tried to hold Max's hands and calm him down, but it was too late. My son's meter had expired. He threw himself into a tantrum, an earthquake, a 7.9 on the Richter scale. I threw open the door, away from the "you're-gonna-pay-for-the-rest-of-your-life" equipment, and the two of us tumbled into the waiting room like a ball of body parts landing at Patti's feet. I'll bet she'd barely had time to open a magazine.

I held Max as he writhed and screamed for the entire hour of our appointment while the speech team did nothing but stand over us and watch. Where was their language? They were speechless spectators at a barroom brawl. I was so humiliated, trying my hardest not to teach Max any new words in the heat of the moment. But Patti stayed true to character, cool, unflustered, never leaving our side. I'm sure she would later recount the episode as just "a bit out of hand."

When we finally left, with the speech team still lined up like birds on a telephone wire, I wondered how quickly we could sell our house and move to another state. What if they send a written report of their observations? And to make it even worse, we'd missed our entire evaluation. I thought these were the people who would help Max communicate. On the way home we stopped for lunch at McDonald's. That had been my promise to Max if he would simply, "please" I pray, get into that dilapidated rickshaw of a getaway stroller and leave the scene of the crime.

Max was a completely different child when we entered through the sacred gates of McDonald's Playland. He bounced up and down in the ball pit laughing as he watched the other kids shooting out of the tube-like slides as if it were a giant vending machine. When Max wasn't consumed by fear, he would explode with joy. Patti and I sat together at a plastic table, watching Max and breathing in the distinctive scent of rubber floor mats, dirty socks, and cooked onions. There was an uncomfortable silence building between us.

Finally we locked eyes, the truth of our struggle fluttering in the stale breeze. I expected her to tell me that this wasn't a gift after all, but there was only silence. And yet there was something so genuine in her eyes, gentle and knowing, almost hopeful, as if we were moving toward something rather than being pulled away. Patti and I sat alone together picking over Max's cold french fries, dipping them in ketchup, and savoring them as if they were shrimp cocktail.

PICTURE TALKS

While the experts offered little hope — when I could even get to the experts — we discovered something even they didn't know: a solution I'd been training for my entire life, an answer I needed as desperately as Max needed it. It was a breakthrough, which, in our case, began with something breaking.

It was the last day of school, the start of summer vacation for my eight-year-old. Max woke up in the night. I could hear him talking. I pried my eyes open with the same agonizing force I used every night. Then I heard something new.

THUD. CRASH.

I sat up quickly, fumbling for my glasses. By the glow of the bathroom light I could see into Max's room. There, on the floor, was a lamp lying sideways. And then I caught a glimpse of Max swinging his arm and sending the other floor lamp to the ground. Before I could even clear my throat to speak, Max charged into my room and tore the blanket from my bed, leaving it in a heap on the floor.

"Max! What are you doing?" I gasped, now fully awake and chilled by the sudden rush of night air against my skin.

Max grabbed my pillow and clutched it to his chest. "Downstairs!" he screamed at me, "Go downstairs!"

"Max, it's the middle of the night," I reprimanded as I stood up.

"Downstairs!" he shrieked, shoving the quilt at me. "Take the blanket."

I reached my arms around the white down comforter that lumped between us like a third person. "Max. I'm not going to go down — "

"Take the pillow!" he screamed. "Downstairs!"

As Max pushed the pillow toward me I stood motionless. This can't be, I thought to myself. He remembers what happened a year ago. "Max. We need to — "

"Mom! Go downstairs!"

I stared into his face, his eyes red and terrified. I knew what he wanted; he wanted me to repeat what I had done a year ago when he was taking medication and got so wild in the middle of the night. He wanted me to take my blanket and pillow and storm downstairs again. But all that craziness ended when the doctor took him off the medication. And then it hit me — that had happened on the last day of school, exactly one year ago to the day.

Max was inconsolable.

Reluctantly, I took the blanket and pillow and walked downstairs. When I returned Max was standing in my room, sweat beading on his forehead, staring at me as if he were stranded.

For a week every night the routine was the same. I tried to talk with him, even apologize, but he didn't have the communication skills to understand. I didn't know what to do, but I knew how he felt: desperate to make sense of the world, to put the pieces together, to have control over the bad, scary things that happen. He's exactly like the rest of us, searching in the wrong places for answers, hoping someone trustworthy will show up and help us through. Each night Max and I would play-act the same agonizing scene, the theater of the mad, until Max would eventually let me hold him in my arms. I could feel his little heart pounding, the heat of his body radiating through his thin pajamas, with nothing between us but secrets.

I called one of our autism consultants, Janet McTarnaghan.

"He doesn't understand what happened last year," she said. "And he's associated it with the end of school. He's trying to make sense of it."

"You're right," I answered desperately. "But how do I stop it? I can't take away the medication this time; he isn't taking any."

"Show him what happened," Janet told me. "You're an artist, Emily. Use your gift."

I sat down that day and drew out the sequence of events like a television storyboard with words and pictures. I drew myself walking downstairs, sitting on the couch, and then walking back upstairs. I hadn't disappeared, I explained visually; I just needed a minute to "calm down." I showed Max that a medication was responsible for making him feel badly and that everything was okay now. It was over. I nervously sat beside Max and presented the work as if he were the toughest creative director I'd ever worked with. He was entranced.

That night the problem stopped.

A FEW MONTHS LATER MAX WAS STRUGGLING at his public school. Anxiety was ruling his life, pinning him down like Gulliver on the island of Lilliput. I continued my one fervent prayer: that God would free him, heal him of his fears. And every day I kept vigil for an answer.

While I was waiting for God to fix things, I decided to buy a little time and try more storyboards with Max. I began creating them in front of him, drawing simple sequences of cause and effect, problems and their solutions. I explained what was going on around us at the time. Max was used to seeing me draw and was quick to sit beside me, even making comments and requests.

Then one night, when Max was sitting in the bathtub, he asked me to draw Joanne's blue sports car. I didn't know what he was talking about; his Aunt Joanne doesn't have a blue sports car. But I grabbed paper and a pen, ready to record his words and draw the images he would describe.

That night, as he soaked in the tub, Max told me in full detail about a babysitter named Joanne who had taken him out of our home for the day, without my permission, in her blue sports car. I remembered it too. But Max was barely two years old at the time, a human SuperBall and unresponsive to language. I had fired the sitter when I came home early from freelancing in a design studio and found an empty house. I never considered that Max, at such a young age, might remember this, let alone in the perfect detail he described. He told me about riding in the front seat of her car without a seat belt, the town and street where she lived, and that he had sat on the floor of her blue house and cried. As Max watched his words and images land on the page, becoming real and concrete and valid, his language poured out like water. He was still afraid.

When we finished drawing, I stared at my eight-year-old son, naked and soaking in the tub. What else is in that mind, perfectly preserved? What other secrets has he been waiting to tell me?

We kept drawing.

Every day I would pull out paper and pen and ask Max what *he* wanted to talk about. His language would pour out onto the page as I took dictation and drew the images he was describing. He trusted me with his most intimate thoughts, fears, hopes, dreams, likes, dislikes — all the things I longed to know but until now had been hidden from view. Sometimes his fears were irrational — and yet real and consuming to him. It began to make sense of his behavior, his cries for help, as never before. As he spoke, after so many years of silence, it was as if the entire world held its breath to listen. Even the crickets outside his window were stilled. Together, using the gift of art God gave me so long ago, we gently sifted through his thoughts, these tender secrets, and strung them together like pearls of understanding, gems of truth.

Picture Talks, as we later came to call them, eventually became so powerful that in the midst of a tantrum I could hold out a sheet of paper like a white flag on the battlefield and offer him a peace talk. Max would hold his fire, cease his thrashing, and cross enemy lines to sit beside me and calmly work it through on paper. And he would tell me things I never could have imagined were in his thoughts. He could release his burdens onto the page, trust them to me, and be free. I don't know why I didn't see it earlier; our Picture Talks were lifting his anxiety. In all my years of longing to do something more significant with my gift of art, I never dreamed it would be used to give my child his voice.

Drawing together became like a love note between us, and a love note from God who strings our lives together with just such intimacy. Sometimes God lets us see a little picture of how life makes sense. I would only come to realize, in time, that this was far more of a breakthrough than I could have imagined.

CHAPTER 12

GRIEVING THE DREAM

Picture Talks began to open up Max's understanding of the world, which is exactly what my dad wanted to do for me. Knowing the pressures I was under, he decided that a family getaway was in order. Only this wasn't like the other trips Dad has orchestrated, bringing us to wonderful places, most of which included darling little mints on the pillows. On this particular trip, I wasn't even sure I would *have* a pillow. My dad was bringing my brothers and me to Lima, Peru, so that we could see how most of the world actually lives — in poverty. I packed enough granola bars to survive five days without consuming a single bite of Peruvian mystery meat and, as instructed, brought nothing of value that could be stolen.

First on my dad's agenda were visits to several Peruvian prisons so that we could see how the ministry he founded in 1975, Prison Fellowship, had reached even to these forgotten places. Not exactly your Club Med excursion, but I love to see my dad at work in prison. Something happens to him there, or something happens to the way I see him there. As an artist and designer, I thought I'd been particularly cool during a certain segment of my life, perhaps 25 percent of my life's pie chart, sipping cappuccino with my artsy friends in our slick black clothes and squirting out creativity like toothpaste. But in his wingtips, starched white shirt, and conservative Brooks Brothers suit, my father redefines cool. Dad comes alive, animated, when he visits prisoners. I've watched him throw his arms across a multicolored sea of inmates' outstretched hands like a coral reef of fingers, grabbing for everyone within reach. What I see is the cool confidence of knowing that when he was knit together, every little hair stitched in place, it was for such a moment. God used my dad's lowest days during Watergate, and his seven months in prison, to boost him into his purpose. I remember that often when I feel like a bottom-dweller.

After the prisons, we drove back toward the city of Lima. We passed homes built from sticks and scraps of metal, with dirt floors, the only source of water being an occasional cement cistern coated with soil. We stopped briefly at one of the worst slums to visit a work project initiated by one of my dad's friends.

When we arrived it was nothing more than a one-room cinder-block structure with little heaps of wire and wood and paper lying on a dirt floor. Everything was covered with a film of chalky gray soil. The owner of this recycling center, a man in his forties, stepped into the white sunlight to greet us, anxious to show us the business he had built from a loan of one hundred dollars. And with that humble business he could take care of his family.

What caught my eye were his two daughters who were leaning against a trash cart, watching us. The older teenage girl was captivating, her arms folded across her chest and wrapped around her thin torso as if shyness caused her pain, a story imbedded in her eyes. Both girls were wearing faded clothing covered with stains, their faces disturbingly adult. I pointed to my camera and then toward them, sign language for "can I take your picture?" The father rushed in and put his arm around the younger daughter and walked her over to his wife. We watched as the girl's mother slid aside a sheet of rusted metal and dipped her arm into the cistern pulling up a cup of precious water. Tenderly, in the same way that I smooth Max's cowlick and straighten his collar, she washed the dirt from her child's face and hands before the father brought her back for the photograph.

We covered a lot of ground that long weekend and, to my delight, ended up at a therapy and rehabilitation center built by Christian missionaries to serve children with disabilities.

As we entered through the steel bars and barbed wire, clearly protection from the impoverished neighborhood, the building was as nice and new and clean as the center Max attended for therapy. Seeing the children inside, with their big brown eyes like chocolate coins and jet-black hair, all around my son's age, made me miss Max desperately. I imagined him at home, curled up under a blanket next to my mother who was caring for him, sharing a book together or building bridges out of Legos. These Peruvian children must have wondered why I suddenly rushed at them like a game-show contestant, applauding and praising their work, throwing my arms around them. I darted from child to child, studying their faces, their every gesture, searching. Finally, I had to ask our translator for assistance.

"Could you please ask: where are the children with autism?"

My question came forward in Spanish, and the director of the center, a fairly well-dressed woman, shook her head — no.

"Are there any children with autism at this center?" I repeated.

Again, my words were translated. The director quickly gestured — no.

"Tell her I have a son with autism," I said smiling, letting her know I'm a lifetime member of the club. "He's eight years old."

The woman looked at the translator, and then back at me with her eyebrows down as if there were some third language no one understood.

The three of us went back and forth for five minutes. "*Autismo,*" I would agree with the translator. "Yes. My son — *autismo.* Where are the children with *autismo*?" I made a huge exaggerated gesture, shrugging my shoulders and turning up my palms. Finally the woman began to speak to the translator, who then turned to me. His tone was hushed and final. "She said they don't *have* any children with autism in Peru."

My mind raced. Is that possible? Could it be the diet or climate, or is it really our vaccines? But it didn't make any sense; autism was on the rise everywhere. "They *have* to have autism here," I said, searching his eyes.

The translator looked at me cautiously. "They have children with autism," he said. "But in this community, they don't survive."

WHILE I NEVER ATE THE FOOD, I came home from Peru with traveler's sickness, the kind that kicks you in the heart. I had to do something. I had this incredible urge to tell every parent I knew to hug their autistic kids, to never let them go. So a few weeks after my trip to Peru, I left again and went to the place where parents gather — an annual retreat set deep in the woods of New England.

The primary purpose of the retreat was to pamper parents of autistic kids. Most of us arrived bleary-eyed and exhausted and were quickly spoon-fed macaroni and cheese as if it were medication and offered opportunities to talk and share. It was safe and blissful, sixty mothers and fathers tucked into a rustic building nestled among the pines, bonded by our common experiences.

The last seminar of the weekend was listed on the syllabus as "Grieving the Dream." The idea was for parents to voice all that we expected life to bring when we had our children, all the plans and hopes and dreams that collided with our child's diagnosis. Everyone went to the seminar to grieve the lives they believed autism stole from them. Well, *almost* everyone.

I understood grief; I resented people telling me to "get on with my life" when I was in the midst of divorce and holding an eighteen-month-old baby in my arms. And you can't simply get on with life when your child has been diagnosed with autism. But for *me* this idea of focusing on myself and what I *didn't* have, the imaginary perfect life that *would have been*, sounded about as helpful as throwing myself into an active volcano. It felt so unfair to my precious Max.

And I knew what Peppermint Patti would say; she keeps telling me that Max is a *gift*. So, while the other parents headed to the seminar, I grabbed several chocolate chip cookies, which can be more practical than a GPS, snuck out the back door and headed toward the woods.

A well-worn path led me through the trees to where it was dark and cool. Streaks of sun filtered through the tall pines creating columns of light. It looked as if God were aiming a flashlight down to the earth, watching to see what I was going to do with all of this. Just an hour ago, parents had been canoeing around the lake, their laughter carrying across the water. And I thought about those same parents now sitting in the seminar, focusing on loss.

I should have gone to the seminar, I cringed. The one sure way to move me past my own pain is to help someone else. I came to this retreat to encourage other parents. I was supposed to tell them that there are families, half a world away from ours, whose autistic children never even survive. I had seen such brokenness and poverty in Peru that I couldn't stand to see that same pain in the faces of families here where we have so much.

I thought back to something my dad said to me once when *he* was struggling with pain. It was years earlier, but the image was still vivid in my mind. My dad and I were walking through the halls of Georgetown Hospital. He was recovering from surgery to remove a tumor from his stomach. The two of us looked like opening day of a tortoise race as my father scuffed his sheepskin slippers along the linoleum floor, hunched over, holding his IV pole with one hand and my arm with the other. He was brave, up and trying to walk after nearly losing his life to infection just a few days earlier. He hung on my arm, and I hung on his every word, so grateful to have him beside me. We walked the tiny stretch of hospital hallway even as his legs shook with weakness. "It's not what happens to you in life that matters, Emily," my dad said, his voice faint and gravelly from all the tubes that had been in his throat with the surgery. "It's how you handle it that determines your character."

Twigs snapped underfoot as I pivoted on my heel and headed back toward the retreat center to meet the other parents after the seminar. I don't think this diagnosis steals our dreams. What if it were the very thing to build our character, to give our lives purpose?

WHILE I WAS AT THE RETREAT Max had spent the weekend with his dad, as he did twice a month. I need breaks from the intensity of parenting, and yet even being away from Max for two days made me miss him desperately. Max and I returned home at the same time, and I threw my arms around him, burying my face in his soft warmth. And I thought about Lima, the grief in the hearts of the mothers who had lost their autistic children, whose arms were now empty. It was then that I had a picture in my mind, as if an elevator door suddenly opened, and I could see the faces of all the children I had met in Peru. And I had a tiny idea.

The next day when Max was at school, I went into my basement. I pulled out all the plastic bins I had neatly stacked on shelves and brought them upstairs. These were my treasure chests holding every piece of clothing Max had ever worn, drenched in memories of love. I had never let anything go. And I was sure I never would. I sat on the floor and ran my hands over the soft pastel fabrics, placed his one-piece suits up against my shoulder, remembering how small he was in my arms, the clean earthy scent of his skin, remembering a time before autism was our life. I held the pint-sized khakis he wore on his first day of school, the beautiful sweaters I dressed him in after his diagnosis. These were clothes that whispered, *"This is someone's child. Take good care of him. He is cherished and deeply loved."*

I ordered labels printed in Spanish that read, *Jesus me ama* — "Jesus loves me." For days I ironed the labels into the collar of every shirt and gently folded and tucked them into mailing boxes. I tried to picture the children in Peru, with their black hair and coffee skin peeking out of Max's familiar clothing. I had always dreamed I would have more children to fill them. And indeed, I do. I hesitated before I taped the last box and couldn't help but open it one more time to soak in the memories of my sweet Max. What I saw instead was a label.

Jesus me ama.

CHAPTER 13

THE CIRCLE

It was Terry's birthday. Max was at school, and I hoped there wouldn't be a call telling me to pick him up early. I wore my cutest ladies-having-lunch outfit, jumped into my car, and headed for the restaurant. A huge flowering plant with a fluffy pink birthday bow sat in the passenger seat waving its twiggy arms at me with every pothole. I really needed this break; the challenges of autism were only increasing, restricting us more and more each day, isolating us from others. But lunch with this circle of women from my Bible study would revive me. There is something about praying with others that bonds friendship in the deepest, most genuine way.

It still felt odd to think of myself in a Bible study. I don't think I ever questioned the existence of God; even as a budding young artist I could recognize the work of another designer. Mom had read to us from a children's Bible when my brothers and I were kids, but back then I was much more concerned with the poorly drawn illustrations than the content—a hint of a budding designer more than a committed Christian. It wasn't until several years before Max was born that I decided to take a look for myself. I was curious; my dad had made a complete turnaround because of reading the Bible. And I was searching for more meaning out of life, something to give me a little more tread on the bottom of my shoes. So I started reading one of the only titles I recognized: Revelation. It was the most visually captivating work I had ever read. Suddenly, reading the Bible was exciting, creative, inspiring — hardly the boring stereotype I'd apparently bought into.

I was knee-deep in divorce when I accepted an invitation from Cathy, the woman I barely knew who came with me to divorce court, and joined her Bible study. That was seven years ago. I was still a novice back then, as green as the plant on my seat, when I realized how much I didn't know. The Bible is layered, incredibly complex, and yet perfectly simple. But your heart has to be open to truly "read" it. I suppose at that point in my life my heart had been broken wide open.

In those dark days of separation, divorce, and Max's diagnosis, I knew my faith in God had become real — although I can't point to an exact moment when that happened. It was as if trusting in God placed me in the only possible life-sustaining atmosphere, a spotlight that followed me through the darkness in which I could move and live and breathe and see. As Paul, the pastor of our church, once said, "Our faith in God doesn't remove us from the challenges of this world, but it will equip us to cope with the challenges of this world." Max was only three when Paul baptized me in front of the congregation at our little church.

After joining Cathy's Bible study, I joined another one led by our friend Peppermint Patti and her co-leader, Sarah. These leaders were the cool girls, stylish and confident. Patti was constantly asking new people to join, Christians and not-yet-Christians alike, as if she were planting and picking flowers from a garden, making each one feel chosen, nurtured, and adored. And she gave extra care to the tender young shoots.

At one Bible study held at my house I watched Patti lead to Christ a woman who said she was ready to turn her life around. Patti always sat in our rocking chair, this same Kennedy rocker. I'd brought it into the living room when Max was too big to be rocked. On this day Patti bounced out of that chair so fast that it swung back and forth, its rungs still knocking against my yellow walls, even as Patti knelt beside this woman feeding her the words to pray like a mother nourishing a newborn.

The women in these groups became my help line, my scaffolding. There were times when I arrived feeling desperate and fragile, with the emotional state of paper-thin porcelain. These women would gather around me in a circle, love me, pray over me with their hands stretched out like the lush green umbrella of the rain forest, bringing me back to life.

After dodging the Boston drivers, who clearly have more important things to do than look through their windshields, I arrived at the restaurant with Terry's plant, remarkably still intact. I searched the room to find three of my Bible study friends already sitting at a corner table by the window. It was April, and we could see tulips finally pushing up through the hard ground outside, the noontime sun warming our backs. We sipped Diet Cokes while we waited for both Patti and our birthday guest of honor, Terry.

When Terry arrived, a little late and slightly out of breath, she dropped her purse on the empty chair beside me. "Patti's not coming," she announced, standing behind the chair. "She just called me from her car."

"Oh," one of the women groaned with the disappointment we all felt. "Why not?" we asked. "Where is she?"

"Her doctor called her as she was driving here. He told her she needed some tests. So she turned around." Terry scanned our eyes to see if anyone else might know something more.

"What kind of tests?" someone asked.

"I guess the doctor found something on an exam yesterday and didn't want to let it go." Terry unbuttoned her lightweight jacket but didn't sit down. "She's on her way to the hospital right now."

We all looked at one other. The thought of endive salads and one slice of chocolate cake with five forks left a sour taste in our minds. I don't know who said it first, but we all stood up at the same time, dropped some money on the table for our sodas, and left.

PATTI'S SKY-BLUE EYES MATCHED her hospital gown, more of a paper towel with strings. She looked bashful as we poured into the waiting room and surrounded her. A nurse quickly swept her into the back area, and we followed her like baby ducklings, right past the front desk.

We sat in a circle in the small pinky-beige patient waiting area. Patti went in for a first scan, a second scan, and then again for another angle. One by one the women had to leave to meet their children at the school bus stop. Two of us remained with Patti as the doctor poked his head in the door. "We need to do another scan, Patti. There's something there, some sort of mass on an ovary."

Patti turned her face toward mine and looked so intensely into my eyes that I thought I might break in two. I couldn't breathe. The three of us locked hands as if we were skydiving from fifteen thousand feet, and we fell into prayer.

It was ovarian cancer.

Our circle quickly grew larger, filling up with friends and family, church members and townspeople, yet we kept the same tight grip as that first moment in the patient waiting room. People brought her to appointments, cooked meals for her family, cleaned her home, encouraged her husband and children, and tended her garden. When Patti started chemotherapy, Sarah, our Bible-study leader, shaved her head in solidarity, taking her enviably thick golden strands and spinning them into a wig. Patti wore it like a little crown of friendship.

I held prayer meetings at my house. Twenty to thirty of us at a time knelt on my living room floor as Patti sat in the center. We poured out prayers, sang songs, read Scripture. We prayed for healing, stretching our hands toward Patti like a morning glory blossom folding its petals inward at the close of day.

She became more beautiful without any armor, even when she became pale and ill and when her hair and eyebrows and eyelashes were gone. It was as if cancer peeled away the layers that blocked the full view of God's grace and strength. And in our Bible studies she took off the hat and wig and scarf and taught us about Jesus garbed in all the bold shining splendor of her faith.

WHEN CANCER TREATMENTS BECAME too costly, our church held a benefit concert one evening in her honor. Every seat was filled and people lined the back walls. Max and I sat on a bench in the lobby, which was the only way he could cope with being in church at the time. I held my precious boy in my arms as the sound of Patti's beautiful singing voice enveloped us like a warm blanket, the same warmth she wrapped around us when we first met her at that church. Patti sang with such honesty and conviction, with such strength through her weakness, that her voice reached up and poked a church spire right through that flat metal warehouse roof. Everyone in the sanctuary rose to their feet, joining her in worship. Occasionally, I could peek into the church to see Patti on stage, front and center. She looked well, her hair grown back a bit and dyed red just for fun, and wearing a stylish navy blue jacket and pants. She could push past the struggle, the nausea, the frailty, when she had a mission.

"I hope you all have some sense about you that today is a God thing," she began, her voice still sounding like music, each word slow and evenly paced. "Today is an example of God providing through his people, how it is supposed to be. But this is not the only way he has provided for me. He has provided for me on the inside too — in my heart." She paused, looking into the faces of her audience. "I am not afraid of this sickness. In my heart I have amazing peace and joy. And in my heart I have no fear of dying. I can't explain to you how he does it, but he has filled me with his hope, peace, joy, and love."

The church grew silent as she glowed in the spotlight and shined it back on us. "I hope in some way that none of you ever have to experience this need, and on the other hand, I hope all of you get to experience this in some way — that is, God providing, God bringing you to the point in your life where you need him." She looked out over the audience as we hung on her words and on the beauty and credibility that God had given her in the midst of her suffering. I know she'd had her moments of anguish, the times she imagined leaving her family, leaving her two young children. No one would ever choose this diagnosis, and yet there was something that Patti didn't want to trade. As if God — working through her illness, becoming real and visible by providing for her needs, bringing her comfort and wisdom, showering her with his grace — gave to her more than cancer could ever take away. It was as if she had been given a gift. Patti gave a coy little smile to her audience, and laid a Southern twang over her Canadian accent: "Now don't y'all go gettin' sick now."

Despite every medical and therapeutic effort and the continuous prayers for healing, the cancer progressed. She was in and out of the hospital, in and out of pain. But she never lost sight of the urgency of her mission. "Help me up," she said to a friend as she lay in the hospital after yet another of the many surgeries. "Help me get to the nurses' station. I need to tell Lucy about Jesus. She doesn't know."

We all tried to see her as much as possible when she became housebound and lay in a hospital bed set up in the middle of her family room. I would tiptoe in with a load of bricks in my heart, afraid I might disturb her. And then her easy smile would tell me it was good to be there. "How's Max?" she would ask, even when she was barely able to speak. I'd try to turn the conversation back to her, but she had no time for that. "Tell me about Max," she'd insist. "Tell me about sweet Max."

She would ask me to read Scripture while she closed her eyes to listen. I tried to read from the stack of index cards, now all dog-eared and soft and scribed in her beautiful penmanship, so many of her favorite verses she kept with her at all times, but my voice wavered and sputtered like a first grader. Sometimes she would let out a little sigh when she listened, as if a warm breeze soothed her body. And a few bricks would drop out of my heart.

I WENT TO VISIT PATTI ONE SUNDAY NIGHT. Cathy went with me and there were several others, family and friends, mingling in the kitchen. The house was always full of people now. It was November, but her husband Nick was playing Christmas music loud enough for a party. Patti loved Christmas. I stood over Patti's bed in the middle of her beautiful family room. Her Bible and Scripture cards sat on the table beside her, and all those quirky found objects her husband Nick had rescued from the dump glistening around her like treasure.

She was so still, her pale eyelids too heavy to open again. "Breathe out me, breathe in Jesus," she would say to me throughout her illness, as she would force air in and out of her lungs. "Less of me, more of him." But now I had to search for her every slow and shallow breath. Her hair, always stick straight, had wave to it now, and fell away from her face the way seaweed flows with an underwater current.

Cathy and I stood on each side of Patti's bed holding her hands, awkwardly fidgeting like schoolgirls at their first dance, uncomfortable with the vivid truth that healing had not come. I wish I had thanked her for all she had given me, but I didn't even know how deeply her words would continue to carve a path through our lives. "Max is a gift," she would tell me with unwavering persistence, even in the face of our greatest challenges. "These children are a gift." Cathy and I just hovered over our dear friend, silently searching each other's eyes for answers.

And then Patti's closeness began to consume me. I reached for her, just as I had reached for Max when he was two weeks old and was so terribly vulnerable, in need of love and care, mistakes and all. I gently stroked Patti's hair back from her forehead and leaned in close enough to feel her warmth. I suddenly knew what to say, what she needed to hear, that her husband and children would be able to go on without her. "Nick and Sunny and Nicky ... are doing fine, Patti," I breathed as her hair slipped through my fingers like threads of silk. "They're going to be okay." I watched her face, hoping she would suddenly open her eyes and speak. But instead the slightest twitch began to press her eyebrows down. She heard me; I know it. She was trying to tell me something, trying to let out that familiar little sigh like a gentle wind through a screen door, telling me she heard my words deep within her soul. I told her I loved her and kissed her forehead gently, swiftly, before the current pulled her any farther away. She died the next day, there in her family room, in the circle of her husband and children.

JUST FIVE DAYS LATER I STOOD at the podium ready to speak. I looked out over the hundreds of people who gathered for her memorial service. The crowd was too great for any local church to hold, so the service had to be held in a concert hall. I thought I might start to shake in front of such a large crowd, caught by exhaustion and emotion and a little stage fright. But then, in the blur of the audience, I found something I didn't expect to see; I found faces. I could pick out friends from the Bible study Patti led, nurses who cared for her throughout her illness, musicians who sang with her at church, people from different churches and surrounding towns who came to visit her, the woman with a wide smile whom Patti had prayed with as she gave her life to Christ. The circle had grown larger and stronger, stemming from the seeds Patti had planted in her life and the grace we witnessed through her death. It was as if a different kind of healing had taken place, a healing in the hearts of those who encircled Patti. We would go on; the one Patti led us to had never left our side. I smiled out over those familiar faces, all the flowers of Patti's garden, poised to bloom and twist their tender young shoots upward toward the light.

CHAPTER 14

A HOLE IN THE WALL

There were times I couldn't have found the strength to stand at Patti's funeral and speak, times that I could barely stand at all. Her death came at a time when I didn't have many coping skills left in reserve. No one would have known that I wasn't coping well; even in the most gut-wrenching moments I could appear calm and composed, very Queen Elizabeth-like, my head up, smiling to the crowd. I'd been well trained. If Max ever sensed the tiniest deviation in my mood, anything slightly to the side of perpetually positive, he would fly into a tailspin tantrum. I was his stability, his only barometer for reading the climate of the world around him. So I learned how to pull myself up, tighten my guitar strings, and only play the high notes. That is, until Max was in bed, and I was alone.

Falling into my familiar Kennedy rocker, I felt as if all the bones had been removed from my body. I was struggling to catch my breath somehow. I desperately needed stillness, to muffle the noise of life the way falling snow quiets the world. And then I would find the smooth yellow wall of my living room, a place for my eyes to rest, a place to let emptiness wash over me and make it all stop.

But on this night I couldn't turn off my brain.

Autism, for all its challenges, wasn't my biggest struggle. It was the fighting that was destroying me, the unending battle to get the right education, to find the right treatments, to seek out specialists, to pay for all this. I was constantly working to help others understand Max, to see the precious child hidden behind the unpredictable behavior. And every attempt hit a brick wall, or spurred another fight.

And now we had lost one of our biggest cheerleaders, our Peppermint Patti. She would listen, give me sound advice, patch me up, ladle prayers over me like warm soup before I went back out into the snow. I sank deeper into the rocking chair, resting my eyes on that yellow wall, trying to stop thinking, to stop feeling.

But my thoughts keep coming back to one thing, a Scripture: "Get up and eat" (1 Kings 19:5). It kept running through my mind like an endless loop, so simple to remember, such a small request in my tender state. Under different circumstances I'd take it as the perfect excuse to share my solitude with a pint of Häagen-Dazs. Unfortunately, I wasn't remotely hungry. But I think the Scripture is about more than food. It's about taking the smallest steps, with the tiniest effort, to take care of myself. But there is a condition — first, I have to get up.

So I took a deep breath, pushed against the armrests, and lifted myself out of that rocking chair like someone whose body cast had just been removed. I stood there for a moment, listening for the *Chariots of Fire* theme song. But there was only silence, Max finally asleep in his bed upstairs. *Clean*, I told myself, as if I were programming a robot. Cleaning is as mindless as eating, but you can still button your jeans in the morning. A clean house always makes me feel better.

I made my way to the hall closet where I keep the cleaning supplies. But as I opened the closet door, one of the shelves that hung on the inside of the door fell, sending bottles of spray cleaner crashing and bouncing against the floor.

That finished me. All my frustration and fear and hurt spilled out as well. That foolish closet door had opened the floodgate. I was in grade school again, getting picked on by the neighborhood bully, and finally fighting back with all the strength my scrawny little arms could muster. I took that door and swung it open as hard as I could. With a crack of thunder the rest of the bottles flew like bowling pins.

Glass cleaner shot to the left; paper towels unraveled to the right. Aerosol bottles rolled in every direction. It was an enormous mess. I stood there shaking, breathless, hoping the noise hadn't wakened Max — and everyone else on the street.

A FEW DAYS LATER I still hadn't had time to fix the shelving, but I noticed something else that had broken in our house — right in the middle of the wall. I rolled my eyes and thought, great, now how am I going to fix that? Max's rambunctious play habits and poor coordination often took a toll on our older home: he would knock into furniture and drop heavy toys that dented the wood floors. An occupational therapist who made home visits to work with Max once called all those bangs and scratches "character marks." It made me smile and feel a little better about the gentle patina covering every surface. Of course, Max and I were both responsible for jumping together on my bed so often that it completely caved in, which was a worthwhile sacrifice. But this new damage was considerably more than a dent, much more than a character mark, and left me perplexed.

I took Max by his soft little hand, walked him over to the evidence, and pointed. "Max, what happened here?" I asked more out of curiosity than a reprimand. There was no response. Perhaps my language was too complicated, the question too open-ended, so I tried again. "Max, what did you bump this with?" Still no response, so I took a different approach with my interrogation. "I bumped the wall with …," I began, my voice rising at the end and leaving room for Max to finish the sentence. Max walked away as if he didn't even see the perfectly round hole punched right through the wallboard.

My curiosity piqued, I had to figure it out. I searched his toys for something just the size of the hole but couldn't imagine how Max could have hit the wall with such force. This would take the arm of a Red Sox pitcher to punch that kind of hole in the wall. Maybe he hit it with the handle of his beloved vacuum, I thought. He loves to take out the Hoover and carry it around the house. I actually think he loves his collection of vacuums more than any of his toys. As I slowly opened the door to the cleaning closet, all the way open, I watched the doorknob fit perfectly into the hole in the wall. The beautiful wall I plastered by myself when I bought this house. The wall I painted myself four times before I had the perfect hand-mixed color.

The wall I had punched that hole through when I swung that closet door open in my tantrum.

Queasiness filled my gut, and a thin tingling came over my skin that only happens when you desperately want to rewind time. How could I so quickly blame Max when this was my own doing, my own outburst, my own inability to cope with this world?

I walked right over to Max, who had already returned to building the intricate Lego bridges that could only come through a mind colored by autism. I knelt down on the floor beside him, so humbled, and kissed his warm smooth cheek. "I'm sorry Max," I whispered softly into his ear. "You didn't bump the wall. *Mommy* did." He looked even more confused than when I showed him the hole, but he kept his focus on his creation. I sat on the floor with him and the two of us worked quietly together building bridges until the day faded into evening.

That night, when I tucked Max into bed and came downstairs, I returned to the hallway to assess the damage. I'm sure I have a patch kit and plaster to fix this, I thought. I ran my hand against the smooth wall until my fingers hit the chalky cracks around the dark hole. White dust covered my fingertips and plaster crumbled under my touch. And I began to crumble too. I had much more to fix than this wall. I stumbled over to my rocking chair, my nightly refuge, and sunk my face into my hands.

I thought back to something that happened to me years ago when life felt as hopeless as it did right now. Max was only two years old; we were alone and afraid. I was facing divorce, facing Max's increasing needs, a move, diminishing work opportunities. It was a time of gasping-for-breath desperation, of pain that had gone from emotional to physical. Everything was warring against us, even groping to tear Max from my arms. I was fighting with every ounce of strength, holding on to a thin thread of hope like a rope tow to God. One night I threw myself over the end of my bed, hollow, shattered, and began to pray. And the most unexpected thing happened. I got an answer. I knew it was God because he told me something so contrary to my own thoughts, and so distressing that I immediately stopped praying and threw my eyes open.

Jesus wanted me to take his hand and walk with him.

It was beautiful and startling and breathtaking. At the same time, I wanted him to have some sort of magic wand to poof my life back to perfect. What I had prayed was for my precious child to be with me, for him to be safe and well. I prayed for a home and finances and food and work and friends and hope. But walking with Jesus was, by all means, a stunning offer. This wasn't the red type on the pages of my Bible; his presence was palpable. He had somewhere he wanted to take me, walking forward, together.

As Christians, we long to hear from God when we pray, or so I thought. So, just between you and me, I didn't handle this particularly well. I should have responded with a resounding "YES!" screamed from the top of a mountain with my arms stretched out like Maria in *The Sound of Music*. But my response was not so film worthy. It's just that my maternal instinct was in overdrive. "Okay," my willing heart quickly responded. "I'll have to get Max first." And this is where it all fell apart. It was his response to me, so contrary to my instincts, that sent me into a panic. "I'll take him later," he told me, still asking for my hand. Later? You mean separate from me? I was horrified. My arms were soldered like iron around my precious little two-year-old. I helped Max with everything. He went with me everywhere. Why couldn't Max go along with me, bouncing on my hip, as I walked in faith? But Jesus had a different idea. Jesus had a hand, and a plan, for each of us.

While I didn't have a Maria moment, I can look back knowing, in my inmost being, that God has never left our side. In times of betrayal and disappointment and exhaustion, when I've felt like giving up, his hand has been there, giving me something solid to hold on to. God's fingerprints are all over our lives.

And so that night, sitting in my rocking chair, with the chalky white plaster dust from my broken wall still on my fingertips, I made a decision. I took a step, an enormous one-inch running broad jump of a baby step. My friend's death has shown me how brief life is. I don't know how I'm going to do this or how our circumstances are ever going to change. But I think I can find the strength to make one day different, to savor tomorrow as if it were my last. It's not exactly a complicated concept, until you desperately feel like backing out. But unfortunately, life is not as simple as a car wash.

I AWOKE THE NEXT MORNING, as always, to the sound of my son's voice. He was reciting a movie. It was Toy Story I finally decided, a choppy, monotone version of his Disney favorite. Max could memorize an entire two-hour film after only a few viewings. He wasn't talking to anyone, exactly, just enjoying the memory — aloud. It always surprised me that Max woke up autistic, as if he should start his day as a typical child and only slip into his strange quirks and unworldly thinking once he'd had a good breakfast, and I'd had enough coffee. Or maybe, even years after his diagnosis, I was still surprised by autism. Max would look so peaceful when he slept, so beautiful, as if nothing could ever enter his world that didn't match such innocence. I listened to Max's soliloquy for a few minutes with my eyes closed, adjusting once again to the diagnosis.

And then I remembered my decision of the night before. My eyes popped open and the morning light flooded my mind. Before I let myself think another thought, before I let myself move, I said aloud,

"This is my last day alive." I felt a little rush come over me, part fear, part adrenaline. "How am I going to spend it?"

Pictures popped into my mind, my own movies to choose from and savor. I imagined taking Max to the beach and running into the water, with our shoes still on. And then, we would attend the international trampoline-jumping contest, which would once again be held in our backyard, with Max and I as the two lucky finalists. And then we would build Lego bridges together, not the little ones we usually make, but one that spans the entire length of our living room. And maybe we'll go somewhere today, even somewhere daring, like into the heart of Boston together. If it's my last day alive, who cares what others think if it doesn't go well? On my last day, autism is not going to hold the two of us hostage.

I thought about people who have been kind and caring, people I love; I need to tell them so. I'm going to stop wasting energy trying to teach Autism 101 to people who never wanted to attend that class in the first place. I'll still do everything I can to help my son learn and advance, but on my last day alive I'm going to stop handing out oars to people who don't want to row. It's time to throw out my ideas of what I thought life would be, should be, and let joy fill up those brand-new vacancies.

I sat up and swung my legs over the side of the bed. I won't get another day, I thought, and then again, maybe I will. If I do, I promise to wake up the same way, believing it's my last. Don't waste it. We're going to get up and eat. We're going to get up and live.

I stuffed my feet into my slippers and started to sprint into Max's room to kiss him like there's no tomorrow, but stopped just short. And what I will not do today, I vowed, is fix that hole in the wall. I'm going to leave it there as my reminder. I guess I'll have to call it a character mark.

Then again, if we really are going to go see the world, I'd better put the teensiest piece of masking tape over that hole. Otherwise my sweet boy will be dropping the car keys into it.

CHAPTER 15

ORDER FROM CHAOS

With a change in outlook as refreshing as a Nestea plunge, I was ready to dive into our new lives — or at least into a new day. And we had the perfect weather for our first adventure. The sky was blue, the air was warm, and the butterflies were soaring freely through my stomach. But I wasn't going to let a little nervousness stop me. I was channeling Rosa Parks, feeling bold enough to move to the front row of life, even to put on a swimsuit in public. As of this day, we were officially members of the club where all the fancy people in town belonged, and we were going swimming.

Getting Max into the water was easy. Getting him out was another story. I reviewed the rules with him ... again: "Be a good listener; 'you-know-what' goes in the toilet, not in the pool; and when Mom says it's time to come out, we swim to the ladder and walk right out." Max was so excited as he stood on the pool deck that he was vibrating, waving his arms and bouncing on his toes like he was doing a dry-land dog paddle.

Finally, I gave my son the okay and he jumped in. I followed right behind. Although Max was a good swimmer, I stayed close to him for safety reasons, and to be sure, in his enthusiasm, that we didn't crash into other swimmers. Max is never so happy as when he feels the water against his body, when he's floating in weightless pirouettes and ducking below the watery wonderland to explore the blue world of silence. We had a game of looking at each other under water, our cheeks bulging as we held our noses with our hair waving above our heads, before bursting through the surface with laughter.

After a while I looked around and noticed what the other mothers were doing — or not doing. They were not in the water. They were not making dolphin noises. They were not herding their children like an Australian cattle dog. Instead, they were lined up as if posing for a swimsuit ad, reclining along what was apparently the mom wall of the pool, their hair tossed back from their faces, as they casually watched their children from a distance. Compared to me, they looked so 1940s glamorous, as if they might start smoking through long slender cigarette holders. I scanned the lineup, and there in the middle found a familiar face — a woman I had met at a party in town.

Clearly, I needed to relearn a few social skills if we were going to fit into this club. I should say hello, I thought. Max doesn't actually need me beside him *every* minute. He's a good swimmer, and we're in the *shallow* end. "I'll be back in a few minutes, Max," I told him.

As soon as my hand hit the cement edge of the mom wall, I was pulled to it like a magnet. I reintroduced myself to this woman, and we began to talk.

"Is that your son?" she asked.

"Yes, that's Max," I answered, watching my nine-year-old who was now slapping the water's surface to see how big a splash he could make. I marveled at the unfamiliar distance between my son and me, this huge sparkling abyss the size of the Atlantic Ocean. Max looked just like all the other children. "What a great day for the pool," I said as I stood in the waist-high water. I kept my eye on Max as we spoke.

She told me about the ballet lessons her children had earlier in the day and how she would stop to buy chicken at the grocery later. She told me about the color of her new drapes. It was strangely apparent that she wasn't asking about my son's autism, and she wasn't giving me that slow, sympathetic sigh I often get for being a single parent. We made small talk, keeping our lives below the surface.

Normally, I hated small talk. There was nothing small about our lives, and if there was I didn't have time for it. But now, at the edge of the pool, small talk felt refreshing and chlorinated, like the water I was soaking in. I stretched my elbows behind me and casually rested my arms against the edge of the pool. Deep in conversation about where one can buy the most adorable paisley yoga pants, I glanced at Max who was playing in the center of the pool near all the other children. Beach balls were floating through the air, soaring on squeals of delight. And I was trying on the confident glamour of this more casual style of parenting. We were blending perfectly. This was my own private focus group confirming that we belonged. If I had a third hand I'd have used it to pat myself on the back. I tipped my head to catch the rays of sun and decided that joining this club was a very good thing indeed.

Out of the corner of my eye, I saw something large soar high across the length of the pool. I was immediately relieved that it hadn't struck Max. I wouldn't have looked were it not for the exceptional "splat" sound it made when it landed against the pool deck. It must have been a beach ball, I thought. "No," my brain whispered, "beach balls don't splat." A pool toy? I guessed again. "No," my brain corrected, "pool toys don't splat either." I craned my neck upward until I could see the far side of the pool deck where the bright red object had landed. In an instant, all those butterflies swarmed back into my stomach and screamed, "Only bathing suits splat."

I turned my eyes toward the center of the pool to see my son jumping for joy and showing his newfound freedom to the world. His wet bathing suit, which had been launched across the pool like a dripping missile, lay some thirty feet away. Mothers stopped talking. Children stopped playing. Even Lady Godiva would have been shocked. I was ready for the spotlights to come up like a prison break and the lifeguard to yell through his megaphone, "Would the guilty mother please step forward from the mom wall." I quickly thought back to war movies I had seen as a kid; I could hide under the water for hours if I only had a reed to breathe through.

Out of options and without an actual plan, I sprinted toward my child using my arms to paddle. Max looked so happy, his shiny torso leaping up from the water like Shamu at Sea World, so completely proud of himself. He didn't know he'd done anything wrong. All his refreshing innocence on the inside, his inability to lie or cheat or be intentionally cruel translates to a complete lack of modesty on the outside. It never occurred to me to give him a rule about keeping one's bathing suit on — I thought that was a given. Imagine Max's surprise when his mother wrestled and reeled him in like a slippery fish, abruptly ending our first grand day out. And I'm sure we inspired some interesting small talk.

I KNEW ONLY TWO THINGS: our next adventure should be on dry land and preferably out of town. My world of art could be just the right mix for us — a community that extols the unique, the unexpected, and fortunately for us, the naked. And so, determined to live each day with gusto, we set out again.

I found a parking space directly in front of the gallery's entrance, so I didn't have to walk Max through the busy streets of Boston. I took the keys out of the ignition and reached for the rear-view mirror, angling it toward me. I hope I still look like an artist, I thought, applying lipstick and tousling my blonde hair. Max had shown a particular interest in one photographer's work, William Wegman, thanks to his dressed-up dogs, Wiemaraners, appearing in cameo roles on *Sesame Street*. And the gallery at the Massachusetts College of Art in Boston was promoting an exhibit of his work.

We approached the front desk. An expressionless college girl with multicolored hair and black eye shadow asked me our business. "We're here to see the Wegman exhibit," I said, pulling Max close and resting my hands on his shoulders. "My son just loves his work," I gushed. I let slip an overly enthusiastic mom-laugh. The girl immediately looked down, appalled, as if I had broken some cardinal rule of artsy aloofness. I suddenly felt as if my slick black jacket had morphed into a "World's Greatest Mom" T-shirt — with the Wal-Mart tag still attached.

"Follow the hallway and up the stairs," she directed, using her pencil to point the way. I noticed she had black fingernails.

We wove through the narrow hallways and into the dark recesses of the old building. The only thing propelling Max through this maze was his intense desire to see his favorite dogs from *Sesame Street*: Fay, Batty, Crooky, and Chundo. He even hoped they might be there in the flesh. But when we came to the foot of stairs that led to the gallery and faced the dark and winding staircase, Max's anxiety took over. He froze and began to cry. Time for a jingle, I thought. That will put him at ease. So I started to sing: "Batty and Crooky and Chundo too, all the doggies wanna meet you." Max burst into a smile and began chanting the mantra with me, climbing each step to the beat. When we reached the top of the stairs it felt as if someone bumped the needle off a record. The gallery was pitch black.

I looked around the huge expanse trying to adjust my eyes to the darkness. There in the middle of the gallery was a brilliant white square of light. Slowly, I began to make out shapes, black silhouettes against the white square. I realized I was looking at the outline of at least one hundred people viewing a slide show. They were artists, I assumed, based on the asymmetrical shapes of berets and feathered hats and spiked hair. Every head was turned toward us, and none of them remotely resembled canines.

I dropped my tail between my legs and turned around. A gallery lecture, I thought, why didn't anyone tell me? Max can't possibly survive this. "Chundo isn't here today, Max," I said, hoping he would leave without a fight. "We'll find him another day." If there'd been a banister I would have slid down it. But I slowly descended the dark and winding stairs, holding hands with my slightly uncoordinated son until we found our way past the girl with multicolored hair and out to the street.

We stood there for a moment holding hands, dazed. Cars were whizzing through the intersection, horns were blasting, lights were blinking—just the sort of thing to send Max into a tantrum. I certainly wasn't ready to walk Max down a busy Boston street, at least not without the Russian weightlifting team to assist us. But the thought of returning home now empty-handed, with fifty-three minutes still remaining on our one-hour parking meter, was unbearable. "Come on, Max," I said with my knees buckling. "I know a place close by."

I squeezed Max's soft hand and said a prayer as I heard the theme song from *Jaws* playing in my head. Tall brick buildings fenced us in on one side, while the street whirled with a fracas of trucks and cabs and exhaust. As we started down the sidewalk, several well-dressed pedestrians scurried past us with a gust of wind. I made eye contact with a few, analyzing which ones had been scout leaders in a past life and would help us. "You're doing a good job," I reassured Max. "We're almost there." I looked down at Max, his blonde hair flipping with the breeze as he walked on his tiptoes.

I held my breath as we crossed the street to the only spot I knew within walking distance of the gallery. I let my bangs fall over my eyes and looked from side to side, hoping for anonymity. My big adventure into the city with Max to expose him to art—and I bring him to a hospital? Even when we don't have an appointment? This is humiliating. The breeze swirled up a tornado of labels and stuck them to me like Post-It notes. "You're a failure." "Total reject." "Loser Mom." And I don't even look like an artist anymore.

We walked past the colorful pillars that bordered the entrance, and I was unexpectedly struck with memories. Max was diagnosed at this hospital. We were here with Peppermint Patti when Max threw his terrible tantrum. But when we stepped through the doors it felt safe for the first time, protecting us from the dangers of the city, and the unpredictable chaos of life with autism. I finally loosened my grip and Max darted toward a familiar circular bench in the lobby. I followed, sliding along the smooth wooden seat until I was beside him.

I was so relieved to sit down. I took a deep breath, letting every muscle loosen. Max gazed up at the huge George Rhoads rolling-ball sculpture in front of him, a favorite on every visit. "Ball machine!" Max squealed, as he bounced on the bench. "Ball machine!"

We watched the kinetic sculpture lift colorful wooden balls, drop them onto a mini trampoline, bounce them into a metal track, and roll them in circles like a slinky. Max laughed as the machine kept all the balls moving at once, rolling them in different directions, bouncing one down a xylophone, banging another into a metal gong. It was a jumble of chaotic activity that sounded like a box of kitchen utensils being dropped down the stairs. But as the sounds washed over us, it became music, improvisational jazz, delighting us with its surprising twists and turns.

Other children passing through the hospital for appointments stopped to see the sculpture before moving on: a young boy with a cast on his leg, a little girl with her nose pressed up against the sculpture's glass case. Max was delighted to stay on the bench with me, bouncing on his knees with his arms outstretched and waving like wings.

I studied the sculpture, wondering how the artist had conceived such a complicated piece. As I watched I began to find a pattern, the master plan in order for all things to work together. It wasn't chaos at all. But rather it was precision, every piece in the right place at the right time. And every ball that dropped had a track to catch it and send it in a new direction.

I threw my arms around Max and pressed my nose against his cheek, still flushed from our walk. "Ball machine, Max," I whispered to him and breathed in his childlike wonder.

I WAS FEELING ENERGIZED FROM OUR oddly successful trip to the city, from feeling the rushing undercurrent of order flowing beneath what often appeared to be chaos. But our next adventure needed to be different. It was time to stop shoehorning Max into fancy clubs and avant-garde galleries and let him slip into something more comfortable, more age appropriate, like a brand-new expensive Swedish automobile. Like many kids with autism, Max has unusual obsessions. He loves Volvos with the same intensity he feels for the water, and what he revealed on this next adventure was as startling as anything I saw in the pool.

A cool summer rain beat against the parking lot pavement, the tail end of a tropical storm that had made its way up the coast. As we turned into the parking lot of the Volvo dealership, I could almost feel Max's heart pounding with excitement, rhythmically thumping our car as if we were teenagers driving with the radio at full volume. "Let's go in!" Max shrieked.

We darted through the rain, ducking our heads and sloshing through puddles. By the time we stepped into the wood-paneled showroom, a mere twenty steps from our car, we were soaked. I pushed back my hood and laughed. "We should have worn our snorkels, Max." But my son was single-minded, lunging toward the sparkling white car in the center of the showroom. I grabbed his shoulders, forcing him to wipe his feet.

A receptionist was watching our breathless entrance. "Max, can you tell this lady what you want to see?" I instructed. Max stood speechless, so I bent down and whispered the words into his ear.

"I want to see the new S70, please," he repeated. The receptionist looked puzzled, her puffy platinum hair frozen in place as she stood up.

"We're looking for the S70," I clarified. "I heard it's coming out today." She looked back down at Max, water dripping off his yellow raincoat and pooling on the beige linoleum floor.

"Maybe I can help you," a man said, swaggering toward me with a flirtatious grin. He wore a pale grey suit, and his necktie sparkled as only polyester is capable. "So ... we're looking for a new car today, are we?" I could see another much younger salesman just behind him, ready to pounce.

"Do you have the S70?" I asked again.

"Sure do," he said, gazing at a car with the same glint of obsession I recognized in Max's eyes. "This is it. Just in today."

Max darted toward the car even before the man finished speaking and pressed his nose and hands flat against the driver's-side window. "Actually, it's my son who wants to see the car." I laughed. "He just loves Volvos."

"I can see that," he said, looking down at Max who was stuck to the window like a decal. "I can open the door ... if he'd like," he offered, probably thinking he'd like to pry Max's sticky little fingers off the glass. As soon as the salesman swung the heavy door open, Max wriggled his way inside and jumped into the beige leather driver's seat. New-car scent stung my nose.

"I'm Don," the salesman said with his hand outstretched. "I think he wants you to have this car!"

"Oh, he's ready to buy," I smiled, knowing my son had nothing to offer but a couple of arcade tokens caked with drier lint. "I'm Emily."

Just then I heard Max yell, "Can you get in the car?" The other salesman had been watching Max. The passenger door flew open, and this handsome young salesman wearing a navy blue golf shirt and khaki pants jumped in. Through the back window I could see Max's silhouette bouncing up and down on the driver's seat. I darted toward Max's open door ready to intervene.

"I'm Chip," the salesman said, looking up with a soft smile. Smiling is good, I thought to myself. Maybe we just bought a few minutes. "Do you like this car, Max?" he asked.

"S70," Max squealed.

"That's right. This is the S70." I stared at the two of them sitting in the car together.

"Visor," Max said, looking above his head.

"It has visors," Chip confirmed, reaching up and folding his visor down.

Max did the same and opened the panel on the back of his visor. The mirror lit up, casting a yellow glow on Max's face and hair.

"Radio," Max said looking at the controls.

"Yup. That's the radio."

"There are added safety features on the new models," Don said, trying to engage me again. I get it, I thought. This was a tag-team approach: one salesman babysits while the other goes for the purse.

"Radio on!" Max commanded.

"You wanna hear the radio?"

"Radio on!" Max repeated in his monotone voice and grabbed Chip's hand. Chip pointed his index finger, and Max held on to his wrist as though he were using a tool, pushing Chip's finger toward the button. Music shot out.

"Radio off!" Max yelled, shoving Chip's hand toward the button again, and the music stopped. Max collapsed into laughter, breathlessly wheezing and shaking so hard I thought he might require CPR. His eyes became little slits and his pink cheeks plumped as if there were a gumball on each side. After he finally inhaled, he yelled, "Again!"

I leaned my hand on the top of the open door and laughed with the two of them. Outside the rain beat so hard on the metal roof of the showroom that it sounded like applause.

Through the frame of the open door I watched as this salesman patiently followed every command, and Max hung on each detail of the car as if Chip were pointing to a family album of our Swedish ancestors. At that very moment I fell in love with this salesman, or at least in love with what he was doing.

"Okay, Max," I called, "just one more minute. I think Chip has some other things he needs to do."

"It's okay. I'm fine," Chip nodded. "He's having the time of his life."

An hour later Max and Chip stepped out of the car, looking as if they needed electrolyte replacement and a rubdown. I stared up at Chip. He was taller than I'd realized, in his late twenties, with long, dark eyelashes that rimmed his pale blue eyes. "Thank you so much," I said, which sounded like such a tiny, lowercase cliché. I searched for something bigger to say, something as drenching as the storm outside, but he jumped in before I could find the right words.

"I have a nine-year-old nephew who lives on the Cape," Chip said. "He's autistic too."

"Oh," I breathed. I didn't think Chip had noticed Max's autism; I thought that's why he was being so nice. "Your nephew is lucky to have you, Chip. You were ... amazing with Max," I said, wishing he lived in the apartment attached to the back of our house, which I would begin building immediately. "How is your nephew doing?"

"He doesn't talk as much as Max, but he's doing all right," Chip answered. "I don't see him much." He put his head down a little and looked away, shielding his own story. "It's been hard for my sister."

"I think your nephew needs you. And your sister too." Max was at my side, his face flushed and dewy. "Max," I said, running my hand through his short blonde hair and gluing it back with perspiration. "Can you say thank-you to Chip?"

Chip knelt down on one knee in front of my son, and Max threw his arms around this salesman's neck. "Thank you, Max," Chip whispered as he choked with emotion and closed his eyes for just a little too long.

CHAPTER 16

FALLING UP

Deciding to get off my rocker, so to speak, and leap into life was the wisest decision ever, landing us in unexpected places, with extraordinary people showing up to catch us. And Max was catching the spirit too, eager to spread his young wings and soar through the air. Yet there was still one problem that was beginning to feel like a freefall: the public educational system.

In earlier grades, placing Max in the regular-education classroom had met with some success. But now, in fourth grade, the other students might as well have been managing hedge funds and transplanting one another's kidneys. Max was out of place and overwhelmed, spending much of his day crouching down on the polished white linoleum floor of the hallway and balling up like a caterpillar when someone tried to intervene. In retrospect, I shouldn't have pushed so hard to keep him there.

"I think you should come in," the teacher said to me when she called on the phone. "Max is pretty upset."

"I'll be right there," I told her.

I checked into the office at the school but was told I could no longer walk through the halls without a staff escort. This appeared to be a new regulation, which didn't apply to any other parents. The school wasn't afraid of me physically; just afraid of what I might see, or say, or who I might talk to. But seeing my son was all the information I needed.

Max was slumped against the painted cinderblock wall, his eyes puffy and his skin pale and blotchy as if his internal gears had been spinning wildly all morning. We locked eyes for a moment, but I'm not sure he could see me. I knelt down on the glistening floor in front of him and cupped my hands around his face. "We're going to take ten deep breaths together, Max," I said. "Ready? One ..." I took in an exaggerated gulp of air and slowly let it out. "Two ... three." Max followed my lead and the color came back into his face. Staff members watched like rubberneckers at an automobile accident, helpless, yet morbidly curious.

Three days later I walked the same stretch of painted cinderblock hallway where I had found my son, but this time to once again meet with the staff. I was dressed in my least artsy, most businesslike attire, briefcase in hand, with all my anxieties stuffed down into my dress shoes. I'd prepared a list of questions, and I wasn't leaving without answers.

Mrs. Bauer opened the meeting by saying her staff had "tried everything" to get Max out of the hallway. They couldn't even get him into the special-education classroom, a place designed to serve children with more severe needs. And now there was another problem: Max was socializing with girls. Unfortunately, he had discovered that the best place to do this, outside of a single's bar, was in the girl's bathroom. We all knew his motives were innocent enough, but we were at a loss for what to do.

"I'd like to bring in an autism consultant," I said, my knees pressing against the child-sized Formica worktable as we sat in Max's empty classroom. "We need more expertise with this situation."

Ms. Ryan, a classroom supervisor, jumped in. "We don't see the need for that, Ms. Colson," she said as she pushed her short black curls behind her ear and stared down at her notes.

"But Max isn't learning. We're losing time."

"Our staff is hard at work," Ms. Ryan said and flashed a smile as if it were an infomercial.

"Max is a kid who can learn, but he needs the chance. He isn't even writing yet." I added, "And I think he can. "

"Well, now, that's not true," Mrs. Bauer chimed in with her deep, gravelly voice. "He can write M-A-X."

"Yes, he can, but — "

"Well, I can't see him writing his whole last name," Mrs. Bauer interrupted, her eyes scanning the circle of teachers. "Does anyone see that?" The teachers shrugged. "So," she continued, her plump fingers spinning her pen like a baton, "are we really going to spend the entire year trying to teach him to write the first letter of his last name?" I almost expected a laugh track to kick in.

"No, no," they murmured, shaking their heads.

"At this point," I jumped in, "I believe Max would benefit from the advice of an outside consultant. *I'm* going to pay for it. We need some help with this." I knew the budget strings were pulling at their perspective. And I knew Max was a complicated child, the only student with autism in the entire school. I didn't expect them to have all the answers. I'll even bet they lay awake at night too.

Ms. Ryan looked up sharply, nearly cutting me off. "We feel very confident in the expertise of our staff."

"I just mean ... we need some strategies. A fresh perspective." Unfortunately, the system turns teachers into politicians. If they say Max needs something, then by law they have to provide it. So they're forced to say nothing.

"As I said," Ms. Ryan began, leaning back in her chair and grinning at the other four teachers around the table as if they had been college roommates, "our staff is highly skilled." I expected them to lock pinkies and clink their sorority rings like champagne glasses.

"But ... didn't we just say that Max is still in the hallway ... most of the day? That you've tried everything?" I looked at his teacher for confirmation. An awkward silence hung over the group. "Maybe trying *every*thing isn't the answer. Maybe we should be sure we're trying the *right* thing." I knew I was a gnat in their ear.

"Ms. Colson, *we* are handling the situation." I could see Ms. Ryan's puffy freckled skin getting a little flushed around her collar.

"How?" I asked, leaning into the table and turning up my palms. "What's your plan?"

"You need to understand, Ms. Colson," she snapped. "*We* are the professionals. *You* are the parent. You do your job, and let us do ours."

The room got dark and quiet, and I could feel a giant hammer pounding me into a gopher hole. That comment always silenced me, and they knew it. But there was too much at stake. When I stopped seeing stars, I pulled myself up enough to respond. "As Max's parent ... this *is* my job," I said slowly and deliberately, with laser beam clarity. "It's my *job* to stand up for my son."

They stared at me as if they no longer spoke English.

I know the staff was overworked and their budgets tight. I can even imagine these teachers as once idealistic grad students, ready to change the world one disabled kid at a time, until they fell into a system that removed all the bran from their diets. It's not that parents are always right; we just need to have a voice when things are wrong.

The school requested another meeting, this time in a more formal conference room. They refused to accept additional consultation, refused to allow anyone new to see Max at school. Instead, they had come up with their own strategy: Max would have to leave the public school. They had secured a placement at a military-style boot camp for autistic children. Some children "like Max" have done well there, they assured me. I'd seen the program before, and it was the last place I would ever want my son to be: teachers barking out commands, children following like robots, with no room for individuality, no room for joy and laughter. Maybe some children thrive there, but not *Max*. It would be like locking him in a closet. Something horrid and ugly wanted to burst out of my stomach and eat these people, like in the Sigourney Weaver movie *Alien*.

"We can't send Max there. It's completely wrong for him," I protested sternly. "Don't you remember why he came to the public school? Because when he was in a separate program for autism he imitated all the other autistic kids. It was a disaster. He needs role models. What we need to do is hire someone experienced in autism to work with Max. And find him a quiet space so he's not distracted." I started to feel achy and weak, and my words echoed in my head as if I'd been suddenly hit with the flu. "All I want is for him to be supported in his own school, with the kids he knows."

The answer was no.

I stood up when the meeting was over, papers shoved into my briefcase, in a state of suspended animation. I was as out of place as Max, an artist trying to sculpt myself into the shape of a litigator. I had failed my child. As I left the conference room and walked through the school, I could feel my escort watching me, pulling at my strings as if I were a marionette. My hard shoes echoed through the empty hallway as my feet tapped up and down.

THAT NIGHT I STUFFED MY EMOTIONS DOWN like gunpowder into a rifle and took Max out to dinner. He wasn't ready for a real restaurant, so I chose one strewn with enormous plastic sculptures of cartoonlike characters and filled with other boisterous, wiggly children who were also in restaurant training wheels.

The cook, apparently, also needed practice. The food isn't the reason we're here, I reminded myself as I stabbed my fork into the rubbery chunks. We're here because I made a promise to live each day as our last. Stab. I vowed to grab on to joy no matter our circumstances. Stab. Stab. Vision statements are easier to live by when life turns out like a Hallmark commercial. I used my fork to dig through my food, scratching and sniffing like a cat in a litter box.

I scanned the tables just to be sure there weren't any teachers from the meeting lurking. Max found this eardrum-cracking arcade delightful, and yet one hum from the oven in the kitchen had the potential to send him into orbit. Beside us there were three birthday parties with children yelling and screaming as if they were in a pool. I studied their faces. They were typical kids, the ones who could slip easily into their neighborhood school, coast through life with a glorious C average, and manage the most ordinary things, like childhood friendships. I knew better than to stare; comparing lives is a laundry chute to self-pity.

"Cake!" Max said with anticipation as he squirted out a puddle of ketchup the size of Australia.

"You're right, Max. I bet they'll have a cake at their party." I flashed a smile at Max as plastic as the sculptures.

"Balloons," he said.

"I see them, Max."

I caught the waiter's eye. "My son ordered chips," I reminded him. He stared at me like a dog hearing a high-pitched noise. "You were going to bring him tortilla chips?" I glared. We'd been waiting fifteen minutes; they're not exactly homemade. The waiter nodded and walked toward the kitchen, or perhaps Mexico. But he didn't return, clearly evidence of a conspiracy. "Max," I said, placing my hand on his arm and realizing I was taking an enormous risk leaving his side.

"Stay right here in this booth. Don't move." I started toward the kitchen with a military stride and, ever so nicely I believe, mentioned that my son had been waiting for three days to get a bowl of tortilla chips. And, is there some *problem?*

I felt a hand on my back, our waiter. "And what are we doing?" he said slowly, trying not to startle me. "Is this about the chips?" he asked as if I'd just snuck out of my nice padded room and it was time for afternoon Jell-O.

"Uh … ye-ah," I answered, pulling away from his arm.

He brought the chips a moment later, but Max didn't seem interested. Queasiness came over me, even though I was absolutely right to take control of this, and from now on, *every* situation. I looked across the table at Max. He hadn't noticed that I'd temporarily morphed into Mom-zilla, hadn't noticed me at all. Fortunately, he'd been distracted by the arcade, his milky blue eyes soaking it all in. He was bouncing up and down on the red vinyl seat, his white shirt spotted with circles of ketchup as if he'd been the stunt man in a Wild West movie. His joy convicted me; sometimes he's so beautiful it hurts.

I set some money on the table to cover our bill and picked myself up by the scruff of the neck.

"Max." I smiled. "Let's get a balloon." For the first time all evening, my son looked at me.

"Yes, yes!" he answered. Acknowledge every victory, I reminded myself.

For years Max had been afraid of balloons. Maybe they looked unpredictable, floating when something else that size should drop or bounce like a ball. Just the sight of one could send him into fits of crying and screaming. But through trial and much error we had found a solution, a way for him to conquer his fear and gain control.

Max held my hand as we walked toward the hostess station. "Could my son get a balloon?" I asked the blonde wearing a 1950s-style uniform.

"Sure," she answered, untying the strings.

"Max," I said, "what color?"

He stared at the huge floating bouquet. "Green ... orange ... red," he answered in a mechanical voice.

"Just *one*, Max," I corrected.

But the hostess pulled out three balloons, "He can have as many as he wants."

With the balloon strings twined around my wrist, we stepped outside into the cool night air and stopped on the sidewalk. It had been raining, and the parking lot glistened with puddles and smelled as if the earth had been washed clean.

"Are you ready Max?" I asked as I passed him the red balloon. His skin was iridescent in the street lamps.

"Yes," he laughed.

Max held the string for a moment and an idea popped into my head. This red balloon is my anger, I thought to myself, the venom poisoning my system. "Let it go, Max," I said. He opened his puffy little fingers, and the ribbon slipped right through. Up it went. Max bounced up and down on his toes like he'd been spring-loaded as we watched that red balloon grow smaller and smaller until it pushed right through the clouds that hung in the dark sky and disappeared.

"Gone!" Max yelled.

We both started laughing.

I pulled out the orange balloon and thought, this one is my fear, the noose around my neck. I passed it to Max, mentally gluing all my fears to its surface.

"Okay, Max. Let 'er rip." He stretched his arm toward the sky and spread his fingers like a fan. It shot upward as if it were being pulled, its string waving back and forth behind it.

"Gone!" we yelled in unison, our words chasing it farther away. Our joints went loose with laughter as if someone had bumped us at the back of our knees. It was exhilarating.

Only one balloon left. Why didn't we take more? This balloon is my plan for the future, I thought bravely, the strings I'm holding so tightly, the strings holding me. Summoning all my strength I passed the balloon to Max, with my heart attached. I'm not giving up, I'm giving it over.

"Okay, Max," I breathed. "Let go."

Max held the balloon for a moment, his face filled with anticipation, and then let go. I knelt down on one knee beside him as we held our faces to the sky, breathing in the soft dewy air. Together, we watched the balloon soar up like a homing pigeon. You take it, Lord, I prayed. It's too much for me to hold. I need your plan, not mine. I kept my eyes on the balloon until the night sky swallowed it whole. There must have been a little peephole in the low-lying clouds because it appeared once more, just for a second, as the moon lit it up like neon.

CHAPTER 17

LAUGHING OUT LOUD

I began searching desperately for another autism program, any-thing but the one our public school system had chosen. Every placement was either wrong for Max's needs or filled to capacity. I added Max's name to the bottom of several wait lists, even to a wait list three hundred kids deep for a school called Melmark. If by some miracle they had an opening, it was forty-five miles away, right through the worst of Boston traffic. How can there suddenly be so many children with autism? The public school was pressuring me to find another program or send him to the "boot camp" school. I went from a daytime faith to a praying-in-my-sleep faith. Alone in my car, I drove away after yet another rejection and screamed so loudly that I lost my voice for two days.

I lay in bed one night thinking about how much of my parent-ing life has been devoted to the head-throbbing futility of battling a system. And for all my efforts, Max wasn't learning. Worse yet, he now had labels attached to him — like "noncompliant," "behavior problem," "unteachable" — that gave others permission to give up. I can't let those labels dictate Max's future. I reached over to my bed-side table and grabbed something: a receipt from God.

At the risk of sounding like someone who tries to sell odd things on eBay, like a piece of toast with the image of the Virgin Mary etched in brown crusty bread, something unusual ended up on my roof just one week after Max and I sent those balloons into the air. Yes. It was a popped balloon with the string still attached. Now, maybe it came from a neighborhood party or an open house. But in all my fifty years, the only thing that's ever landed on my roof was our trampoline when a strong gust of wind lifted it from our backyard. When I told my friend Sue about the popped balloon lying on top of our house, she gave me permission to believe in something more. And so, I decided to consider it a receipt, the way you get a card in the mail when you send a certified letter, confirmation of goods received and accepted, something for my spiritual accounting at tax time.

I wrapped that balloon string around my hand and wondered what would happen if I redirected all my energy, stopped trying to get other people to teach Max, and just did it myself. Clearly, this was a thought of the desperate and sleep deprived. I'm not a teacher; I'm an artist. Yet God showed me how to use this artistic gift to reach Max through our Picture Talks. Max can tell me things now over paper and pen. Still, the thought of becoming a teacher made me pull the blankets up over my head. I hid there, imagining myself as the Barney Fife of the educational world, nervously shooting myself in the foot. But if nothing else, it might make Max laugh. Humor has been part of my own survival kit. And my son's laughter, as I learned early on, has helped *him* as well.

I remember Max as a little toddler standing on his big-boy bed, wearing one-piece-footsie pajamas, waiting, watching. This one will get him, I thought to myself as I jumped around the corner singing "What's New Pussycat?" in my best Tom Jones impersonation. When I got to the "whoa-whoa-whoa," with my arms out and hips swiveling, Max disappeared. His bed was suddenly empty. He'd laughed so hard that he flipped backward right over the headboard. I ran around to find him laying face down, eyes closed and motionless on the carpeted floor. I was sure I'd killed him. I leaned in close. He was still breathing. Don't touch him, I thought. He's broken something.

"Max!" I gasped. "Max."

After a few anxious moments, Max lifted his head and his eyes popped open. And for the first time in his life, he looked directly into my eyes. It took my breath away. Then, with our eyes still locked, he began to shake violently, uncontrollably, with the convulsions of a Tickle-Me-Elmo doll.

"Again!" he shrieked.

While we subsequently avoided standing on the bed, I did anything to make Max laugh. I ran around the house and made the sound of someone falling in a manhole, pretended to trip and fall on the floor, piled up the living room pillows and dove into them like a swimming pool. Max would pretend to fill me up with air just to watch me shoot around the room like a deflating balloon. And I made up crazy songs to help him move through his day. Initially, I worried that the neighbors were watching, but I quickly realized they were trying their best *not* to look. I was, after all, working for a captive audience, a focused, connected, interactive audience of one. It was as if laughter and humor bore their way right through the wall of autism. If he was laughing, he was learning.

Of course, Max needs structure and predictability and information broken down into digestible chunks. But maybe it could be creative and fun too. My friend Peppermint Patti once told me that while the artistic right side of my brain is remarkably robust, the left side must look like a shriveled-up pea. It was the chemotherapy talking, one of the drugs our circle of friends called "truth serum." I don't agree, mind you. It's just that the left side is more ... preserved. I could sell it in a yard sale as "hardly used." If Patti were right, it was time to bring in help — someone who loves teaching, is up for a challenge, and isn't afraid to fall down on the job. Literally.

The next day I jumped out of bed filled with excitement and called Lena, Max's aide from a summer camp. Lena was full of fun and had just completed a year as the only female on a men's wrestling team, a most appealing qualification. Fortunately, Lena had a rather large college tuition payment due, and she agreed to work with us several afternoons a week. We already had the funding through a state grant, an emergency relief program of sorts. And Max's father was helping us enough financially that I could devote more of my design skills to creating teaching materials for my most important client: Max. Lena and I immediately fell into a spark-flying rhythm of teaching Max together.

LENA BOUNCED INTO OUR HOME with the same high-voltage energy level as my son, which is enough to power half the houses on our street. I had our games ready and a visual plan for Max to follow. Reading comprehension was first on the list. Max could read surprisingly well, but understanding what he read was the challenge. Lena handed Max the first card with such fanfare you would have thought it was an Academy Award.

He read aloud, "This is the place you go to get clean at the end of the day."

He stood for a moment, thinking, studying the printed words, and then disappeared around the corner. I could hear him reading and laughing before we could catch up to him standing beside the bathtub.

"Do ten jumping jacks in the living room and then look under something blue," he read from another card.

At the time my brother Chris's wife, Cheryll, was teaching third grade in another state, and she inspired me to teach Max in motion, a very good idea for someone with more energy than Ricochet Rabbit.

Spelling was next. Lena grabbed the salad spinner. I threw in a handful of plastic tiles. "Big money! Big money," we screamed as Max spun the letters just as you'd dry lettuce. He spilled the tiles onto the floor and immediately ordered them into a word. Lena and I jumped and clapped like Vanna White. Max was drunk with excitement.

Before we gave Max a break, I ran around the house placing cans of food in all the rooms. "Get your shopping cart Max," I yelled as if I were starting a stock car race. "Ready, set, go!"

Max dashed around the house filling his toy cart with items. Lena met him at the dining room table where they used a plastic cash register to add up his prices and write down the total. Max could do basic addition, until it was a demand, at a desk. But when he was imitating his favorite television show, *Supermarket Sweep*, he didn't even know he was learning. But I did.

Our home program became my encouragement, a handrail to steady myself, as I continued searching for a new school. And Lena, with her unbreakable spirit, became like sunlight in our home. We worked together to continually raise the demands and shape our program into more traditional teaching. Turning our home into a game-show set is hardly the stuff of peer-reviewed research papers, but God doesn't give all the autistic children to parents who are speciald-needs teachers; sometimes he gives them to the rest of us. Even to an artist.

CHAPTER 18

OUT OF TIME

Time was passing. I couldn't find an alternative school program. My eleven-year-old was still dusting the public school hallway with the seat of his pants and enjoying social hour in the girl's bathroom. The public school called me in for yet another meeting. The boot-camp school was holding the opening for Max, they told me, as if it were some sort of favor.

"That school will destroy him," I protested.

"He has to go somewhere."

"But not there."

"Then tell us where *you* think he should go, Ms. Colson," the classroom advisor pressed.

"Well…" I flipped through my list of twenty school visits. "I don't know yet." And with those words I handed them all the control, all the power. But I quickly added, "We have a home program. And I'm watching him learn. I know it's possible."

"Max needs a school, Ms. Colson."

"He can learn at home until there's an opening," I said assertively.

"We're not going to allow that. We've chosen the appropriate placement."

"I've looked at that school several times. It's wrong for Max."

"You've looked at *twenty* programs. At this point, we're out of time. There isn't a choice."

"I wouldn't even be able to get Max to *go* to that school." I looked around at the irritated faces of the staff bathed in the unforgiving florescent light. "It's not like I can just pick him up and carry him in. He's almost my size." I laughed, trying to ease the tension.

"Well, he *has* to go. And if you can't *get* him to go, Ms. Colson, then the court will order him to live there."

Silence filled the room. I could feel my muscles suddenly bulge like Popeye's when he swallows a can of spinach. "Not a chance," I said, throwing my voice across the table with the weight of a shot put.

The classroom advisor looked down at her notes, as she often did when her conscience flared. "That's exactly what will happen, Ms. Colson." And then I noticed something she took great pains to hide: an edge of vulnerability peeking out like an ill-fitting slip.

I LEFT THE MEETING WITH A STAY OF EXECUTION — ten days to choose a program before the school would choose one for me. But I'd looked at every school, every possibility, except fleeing the state like fugitives. And then, three days before curfew, I had a call from Melmark, a small private school specializing in autism. I didn't know then that this was our white knight on horseback. All I could see was that the school was impossibly far away and filled with the most complicated children I had ever seen. But Melmark was our only open door.

I STOOD NERVOUSLY BEFORE one of the public school administrators on deadline day, my arms tight to my sides as if I were wearing a straight-jacket. "Max is going to attend Melmark New England," I told him.

"Melmark?" he jumped in as if I'd lost my mind. "They have a *huge* wait list."

"I know," I said, somewhat bewildered. "Three hundred children."

The administrator stood up and furiously scrambled for his notes. He peered into Max's file to confirm his suspicions and then pointed the papers at me for effect. "That wasn't even *on* the list of schools you had looked at."

"No, it wasn't," I admitted. "Max has been on their wait list, and they *just* called me. They have an opening, and they said Max fits their profile."

The administrator shook his head as if I'd been withholding information. "Have you seen it? Have they met Max?" He pressed.

"Yes," I said with a lump in my throat. "We visited the school yesterday."

IF THE CALL FROM MELMARK HAD COME a moment later, Max and I would have already fled town so fast there would have been skid marks in the driveway. Still, I felt sick to my stomach on my son's first day at his new school. As I brought him into the lobby of the blocky office space, Max crouched into a corner, his face twisting into a gut-wrenching scream. I could see several holes in the plaster wall behind him, just at kicking height. Five staff members quickly crowded around him. And I left my son there, my precious eleven-year-old, lying on the floor surrounded by strangers. I drove two blocks to a Staples parking lot — and cried.

I returned later that day exhausted, my eyes puffy and bloodshot, desperate to know if my son had survived. With great relief I threw my arms around Max as if he'd spent the day harpooning whales from a rowboat.

"He did really well," his teacher said with a soft smile, gently placing his hand on Max's shoulder. "We got a lot of work done today." This guy looks remarkably cool, I thought, for someone who is obviously lying.

"In the classroom?" I cross-examined.

"In the classroom. Max sat at his desk most of the morning."

Over the next few weeks my son appeared to be doing better than I was. He was motivated to get to school, proud to tell me about his day. I was having trust issues, but our first meeting cleared up any doubts. We sat around a long wooden conference table surrounded by walls of glass windows offering a superb up-close view of the interstate: prime real estate from my highway-loving son's perspective, but hardly the verdant, tranquil charm of his suburban public school. I was ready to hear them pick apart every detail of my child, wave his faults in my face like a flag. Or worse yet, tell me nothing.

The educational coordinator opened the meeting. "We're really happy to have Max here," he said. "He's in the classroom, at his desk. He has a lot of good skills." He looked down for a minute and I waited for the catch. There was silence as all the teachers began smiling at one another and nodding as if they actually *liked* my kid. And then he turned the meeting over to Kerri, the occupational therapist.

"I want to talk about Max's handwriting," Kerri said, holding a thick stack of school records in her hands, her reddish hair pulled into a ponytail.

I threw my hand up as if stopping traffic. "I know what the reports say," I blurted out before she could add another word. "It says he can't write. *I know.* But he's made huge progress at home. He's holding a pencil now. He's not anxious anymore." I paused to take a deep breath as the classroom shook with the rumble of an eighteen-wheeler passing by. "I think he's going to write."

"Well, that's great," Kerri said as her face stretched into a wide smile. "Because I *know* he's going to write."

The clouds parted and the angels sang. Even the commuters on the interstate started cheering. I looked around the stark conference room; the hope in the faces of this staff was more beautiful than any tree-lined scenery. We were home.

I wanted to see Max at work, so the teacher let me sit in the back of his classroom. There were six other boys, all around Max's age, with almost as many instructors. And every instructor was fully trained in autism, fully trained in each child's needs.

Max was at his desk with a teacher sitting across from him. "How many blocks, Max?"

"Three."

"And how many blocks here?" Chris asked, pointing to the second stack of colored wooden cubes.

Max used his finger to count the blocks. "Six."

"Good job, Max. Which is more?"

"Six," Max quickly answered.

Chris jotted down Max's response in a notebook. "Are you ready to work on money, Max?"

Max started looking around the room. There were so many distractions: other children working, some having significant behavior problems. I could hear a loud outburst from a student in the hall, and I watched several teachers rush to his aid. No one grimaced. No one even looked flustered.

"Max," Chris repeated gently, "show me you're ready to work."

Max folded his arms on the table, arched his back, and leaned forward trying his hardest to look at his instructor. I thought I was going to melt. "Very good Max," Chris said, as he broke into a genuine smile that matched my own. "Let's do some work."

As I stood up to leave, a teacher rushed up to me. "Let me show you what we've done," he offered. "Max hasn't even tried to walk into the girl's bathroom, and we wanted to ease his anxiety about using the boy's room." I knew that structure and consistency and their obvious expertise were already making the difference. These people took their mission seriously. But as the teacher pushed open the boy's room door, I could see a life-sized construction-paper banana tree taped to the back wall. They all knew Max was obsessed with bananas. I thought I was hallucinating and nearly fell onto the tile floor laughing with the image of all the boys at Melmark standing under the banana tree using Max's tropical relief station. It was close to postcard beautiful.

After he settled into the school, one of the teachers asked if she and several other staff members could take Max out to dinner and to visit convenience stores to "check out the refrigerators." They so *get* my kid, I thought. But then I felt guilty. These teachers never get a break. They work long days year round, changing the lives of the most challenging kids you'll ever meet, yet they're paid less than if they worked in the public schools. Certainly these hip, bright, twenty-somethings have better things to do with their slivers of free time. But Ashley, Max's teacher, began to press like a teenager on a Saturday night. "We love Max," she said. "We want to take him out and have some fun. It's fun for *us* too. Would you let him? Please?" I wondered if selflessness is what makes people more beautiful.

Max began to change and grow and gain confidence. Even the representative from our public school district, someone I'd seen as a threat, was thrilled to see my son succeed and willingly supported his new placement. Max was better able to manage going out into the community, and the walls of our world began to crack open, letting Max's sweet spirit seep into the lives of others in the most startling ways.

One day I watched Max as he sat at our dining room table and held a pencil in his hand. I told myself to memorize this moment, to hold it in my mind as if it were a photograph. Max was trying his best to make his uncooperative muscles behave, to pinch his fingers together around the thin yellow pencil. The point was poised to paper, and my twelve-year-old was writing, or rather, he was trying. There wasn't a hint of frustration as he looked at the page and traced over the letterforms I had lightly sketched. I was close enough to hear the scratching sound of the graphite, to see the glow of his smile. It wasn't exactly the parting of the Red Sea, and yet we had escaped something, crossed into a new place. It was our little miracle.

CHAPTER 19

SUPERMAN

Over the next few years Max made great progress at Melmark and achieved professional status in his ability to venture into the community. And I discovered a talent: Max could see through people. It was as if he had Superman's X-ray vision, revealing the hero and archenemy in each of us. While effortless for him, it was a startling discovery.

After much work to help Max overcome his crippling fear of riding in different cars, he was ready to embark on his first solo adventure with Lena. Max sat tall in the backseat of her Jeep Wrangler, all his teddy bears appropriately hidden in his backpack. To Max, there is nothing more motivating than a trip to the Smithsonian Museum of Appliances, otherwise known as the gas station Mini-Mart. There, under one roof, one can view a microwave, a sparkling display of glass-front commercial refrigerators, and if you're fortunate, a glimpse of a rare dust-coated vintage Electrolux. I can't explain Max's passion; perhaps appliances are simply more predictable than people.

I watched from the end of our driveway as Lena drove away with my son. Suddenly, I realized I had forgotten to share a small yet crucial piece of information: I didn't tell Lena to bond with the clerk. At twenty-something, she might not know the power of a confident smile and greeting to offset the strange rituals of my child as he categorizes the make, model, and temperature setting of each refrigerator.

An hour later, when they finally returned, the two of them burst through the door and Max dashed to his room.

"The strangest thing happened," Lena said as she set their half-empty soda bottles on the kitchen island. "We had to go to a different convenience store."

"Why? Was it closed?"

"No," she said, shaking her head and pulling her long brown hair into a knot. "They weren't very nice."

I sighed. It's the bonding thing. I knew it. "What do you mean?"

"Well, as we're walking in Max said, 'Where's the microwave,' and the clerk jumped on him. We'd hardly even walked into the store and she goes, 'We don't have one,'" Lena said, imitating the woman's snide voice. "So then, Max said it again. 'Where's the microwave.' And the clerk looks at me and says, 'I told him. We don't have one.' She was really rude."

I could tell Lena was flustered. "Oh," I sympathized.

"So then, we walked over by the refrigerators. Max starts jumping up and down and looking inside … *you* know," Lena laughed. I had the picture; I'd seen it a thousand other times. He makes the contestants on *The Price is Right* look like they're on Valium. "He wasn't doing anything wrong, and the clerk yells at me, 'Don't let him touch that. Hey, what's he doing?'"

"Oh, no."

"So I said, 'He just wants a soda.'" Lena laughed, shrugging her shoulders at me. "What was I going to say? We just came in to *look* at the refrigerators?"

"Is that where you got the soda?" I asked.

"No." Lena shook her head. "We got them somewhere else. But there's more. So Max is looking at the refrigerators, and I'm asking him which soda he wants, like that's what we're doing there. And then she said it again, 'Don't let him touch those doors. Why does he have to look inside?' I didn't know what to do, and there was this other lady, another customer, up at the counter buying a candy bar, watching the whole thing."

I'm cringing now, listening with a scrunched-up prune face as if something were about to land on my head. "Did Max know she was mad?"

"I don't think so, but I figured we needed to get out of there. So I put my arm around Max and said, 'Come on, Max. Let's find a different store.'" Lena imitated the exaggerated happy voice she'd used with Max.

"Did he leave?" I asked, knowing how difficult it is for Max to transition from one place to another, especially if appliances are involved.

"Yeah, he started to walk out with me. But then this lady, the other customer, kept staring at us. The clerk was holding out her hand waiting for the money, when the lady turns, pushes the candy bar away, and says to the clerk, 'I think I'll find a different store too.' And then she walks over beside us."

"You're kidding."

"No. She walked out of the store with us. And the clerk is just staring at the three of us. She didn't know what to do." Lena had a huge, beautiful smile as if she were about to explode.

"The other customer walked out with you?"

"Yeah. But it gets better. Just as the doors are about to close behind the three of us, Max sticks his head back inside and says to the clerk, 'You could learn from me.'"

"What? Where did he get that line?" I said, stunned.

"I don't know, but we're still in the doorway, where the store clerk can hear us, and the lady with us turns to Max and says, 'You're right. We can learn from you.'"

I'VE BEEN FASCINATED BY THE WAY strangers react to Max. He brings out the best and worst in humanity, from the rudest of remarks to the most genuine acts of selflessness. No one remains neutral. I learn a lot about people when I'm with Max, like the Volvo salesman who was drawn to Max's joy or the stranger I met in a grocery store one day who was drawn to Max's needs. While everyone else in the store avoided us as Max lay on the floor in a tantrum, one woman didn't walk by. She stayed beside me until I thought of a way for her to help. She made me feel like we're all playing on the same team.

This talent Max possesses, the ability to turn us inside out and see right through us, isn't limited to strangers. He sometimes turns that X-ray vision on his mother. Unfortunately, I don't carry Kryptonite to neutralize his powers.

Max had an appointment with a doctor who specialized in integrative medicine. He wasn't one of those crystal-worshiping, incense-burning practitioners, but a rather sophisticated doctor utilizing both alternative and conventional practices. Max was anxious about walking into the stark examination room, and I was thankful to have my mom with us so that she and Max could sit together just outside the door. Besides knowing Max was cared for, it gave me the opportunity to speak with the doctor without interruption and tell him about the many interventions and therapies Max was receiving. He needed Max's treatment history, and of course, in the process, he would realize I was not a neglectful crackhead parent, but a serious overachiever-type mom. The cross hanging around my neck would speak of my faith, my commitment, my clean lifestyle. I even found a way to tell him that I'd spoken at several area conferences, just in case he might need such a service. All those years as a graphic designer creating corporate identities taught me the power of communicating the right image. I pictured this doctor eventually inviting us into his home, telling me of secret cures for autism, while he stood at his kitchen counter mixing Chinese mushroom powder into wheat grass. And he would realize that helping Max, the innocent child of a loving Christian and by-no-possible-fault-of-her-own single mother, was his life's mission.

"Does he have any language?" the doctor asked as Max sat silently outside the door.

"Oh, yes. It doesn't come easily, but he uses full sentences now," I answered.

He fired off a list of questions about sleep habits, diet, digestion, but kept coming back to the issue of language. "You said he *does* speak, is that correct? He's right outside my office door, and ... I don't think I've heard him say anything."

"Yes, he's just very anxious here," I explained as if we were colleagues.

Our appointment was nearing an end, and I was pleased at the doctor's willingness to order numerous laboratory tests. "Could your son come in so that I could talk with him a bit? Would he do that?" he asked.

"Maybe," I answered. "Max," I called as I looked into the hall. "Can you come sit with Mommy for a minute? Then we'll be all done and do something fun." Max stood up as if he always followed my requests and entered the examination room. The doctor greeted him, but Max brushed past his desk and stood silently at the window gazing out over the Cambridge neighborhood. "Good job Max," I proudly commended. "We're going to do something fun next."

And then it happened. My son must have a locator device implanted in his brain, because it only took him two seconds to see into a storefront window on the street below that obviously had commercial refrigerators. And with that motivation, my son spoke his first, and what would be his only, words for the doctor to hear.

"Mom, after this we can go to the liquor store."

Delighted at the prospect, Max walked out and sat beside my mother, who looks as much like an alcoholic as Mary Poppins.

The doctor's eyes shone on me like headlights. I was so busy being perfect that I forgot to laugh. The more I tried to explain, the worse it looked; he wasn't buying the whole refrigerator-obsession thing.

I HOPE I'VE LEARNED A BIT SINCE THEN, that "perfect" isn't approach-able. It isn't even likable. A friend once told me that he wasn't com-fortable talking to me when he thought my life "looked perfect" because his life was filled with cracks and flaws. And it's the vulner-able beauty of my child, with his seeming imperfections on display, that can permeate even the toughest of individuals and change them right before my eyes.

Max and I had just nestled into a booth ready to enjoy an evening out in a real restaurant, one without a ball pit in the center. It's a skill we'd worked hard to acquire. Max had his restaurant cue cards laid out on the table to remind him of the social expectations such as stay-ing in your seat, giving other people space, and using a voice volume lower than that which has historically shattered crystal. The restau-rant's Australian décor tickled Max as he looked around searching for koala bears.

"I'm Mike." I looked up from my menu and saw a towering figure with short, spiked hair. He looked like a bodybuilder with a bright blue shirt that was tight enough to be a tattoo. The thin, round serv-ing tray, which he suspended with his fingertips, looked out of pro-portion, like a flying saucer hovering over its mother planet. "Can I get you something to drink?" he asked.

"Sure," I answered. "A seltzer with a lime." I waited for him to ask Max. He didn't. "Max, what would you like to drink?" I asked.

"A lemonade," he answered. The waiter stared at me until I trans-lated Max's garbled articulation.

Mike brought our table settings and put both of them in front of me. He came back with some napkins and then with a basket of bread. Again, he gave everything to me. This is new, I thought. Usu-ally people stare at Max, more out of curiosity than intentional rude-ness. Yet this waiter hasn't looked at Max once.

When Mike returned with our drinks, Max excitedly reached his hand out to grab his lemonade. But Mike didn't pass it to him. Instead, I watched our waiter take a step backward and finally look at my son.

Mike's eyes began to bulge and his lip curled. You would have thought he'd been asked to hand-feed a crocodile. Keeping his distance, Mike stretched the drink toward Max. When their hands met on the glass, Mike peeled back as many fingers as possible without dropping the lemonade. And then our waiter groaned. Loudly. "Oh … whoa — wow," and walked away.

I wanted to wipe down my son with antibacterial gel.

The waiter's exclamation was loud enough for the tables around us to look our way and stare. Even with Max's history of earth-shattering tantrums, not once has he ever been *intentionally* cruel. Unlike the rest of us, he's not capable of such malicious thought; and they *actually* call that a social impairment. Max couldn't even recognize the waiter's social slander. He just kept bouncing up and down with excitement, rejoicing at our night on the town, and taking in cool sips of pink lemonade.

I took a hard swallow of seltzer and reminded myself of two things: one, self-control is a fruit of the spirit. And two, this waiter is the size of an apartment building. Both seemed logical reasons not to mention the incident. And then I remembered a third reason: my brother Wendell wasn't with us in the restaurant. I don't often get angry, but years ago I'd nearly lunged at a man in a bowling alley who was there with his grandchildren. He had pointed to my son and said, "Why did you have to bring 'it' here?" and then raised his hand in a gesture to swat my son away like a mosquito. I jumped on a chair like an animal trying to make myself look bigger and snapped out a clever retort, when I felt a little pull on the bottom of my jacket. My brother was gently urging me to come back down to earth, to let his ignorance go.

Mike returned with a pad of paper and pen. Let's start over, I thought. This waiter isn't anything like the bully of the bowling alley. Perhaps I simply misread his signals. I'm sure he'll ask Max for his order and everything will be fine. But he didn't. Max tried his best to order his dinner, but Mike just stared at me as if my son were talking from behind a glass partition.

I gathered all the subtle disapproval I could muster and said, "My son would like to order his *own* dinner, if you wouldn't *mind* taking a minute." Unfortunately I have pleasant PTA mom stamped all over me.

"Oh," he said without any option but to turn toward Max. "Uh … okay." Mike held out his pen and stared down at his pad. "What can I getcha?"

Max placed his order and the waiter left. I'd lost my appetite. It's not that the situation required an apology exactly. I just wanted him to lift the barbells he had casually tossed across my chest. I reminded myself that were it not for Max in my life, my precious teacher, I wouldn't know what to do either. The restaurant was busy, and our waiter was rushing from one table to the next. I watched him, trying to compare his interactions as he served other parties.

A few minutes later Mike walked toward us holding a tray of food for the table beside us. Before I could eavesdrop on his interaction skills, Max yelled to our waiter in a much-too-loud and socially inappropriate voice, "Good 'ay mate!" I flashed my eyes toward the waiter's tough exterior and I saw something crack. Out of the corner of his eye he looked toward Max — and smiled. I leaned into the table giggling.

The waiter served the sizzling dishes and disappeared. A moment later he returned with a lemonade in his hand. "Thoughtcha might like a refill, Max." I stared up at Mike's muscle-bound torso, making sure it was still him. As he walked away I scanned the restaurant to see if someone was holding a remote control and had just changed the station. Max sipped his lemonade and Mike approached our table once again, this time with his hand up. "High five buddy," he said. "Your food's on the way." Max reached up and their two hands met midair.

CHAPTER 20

JUMP IN

I've never seen anything like it. Just as the driver opened her car door and shifted her weight onto the parking lot pavement, a teenage boy built like a refrigerator dove past her and landed flat across the front seat of her car. He went completely airborne for a moment. Typically, one would consider ours a safe town; gang members here wear Dockers with monogrammed belts and loiter at the sailing club. Yet the driver of the car, Mrs. Woods, as she would later introduce herself, watched this apparent carjacking as if it happened regularly.

"Oh-no-Max-no-no," I cringed, darting into the car and groping for my child. "I'm so sorry! He's my son. He just *loves* your car."

"We do too," Mrs. Woods mused with a smile.

I laughed breathlessly, with the look of one watching a horror movie, as Max refused to budge from her front seat. "Max! You can't do this!"

"This has been a great car," she said introspectively.

"I'm *really* sorry. It's just that his grandfather used to have a car exactly like this one," I cried with pleading eyes. "Same color. Same seats. Same year. Everything."

"Hmm. Does he think it's his grandfather's car?" Mrs. Woods probed thoughtfully as if Max were in psychoanalysis.

"Oh, of course! That *must* be it," I lied, turning to my son. "Max, this isn't Grandpa's Audi. You have to come out. Right now!" *Of course* my son knew it wasn't my father's old station wagon, the one he'd sold a few years ago. Max could have identified that car right down to the tiniest birthmark. Max had spied this car, a near duplicate, while driving around town. Every time we'd pass it, Max's head would pop up from the backseat like a periscope, and he'd yell, "Mom, we have to follow it!" We never did follow it for the very reason in front of me now: my son glued into a stranger's car so tightly that it would require the jaws of life to remove him.

"Mom! Get the camera!" Max squealed. "Take a picture!"

I fumbled with the camera, self-conscious that I had already clicked a photo while no one was looking.

"Right," Mrs. Woods offered calmly. "You *should* have a picture."

I love people who don't treat all of life as a fire drill, probably because my mind is often dreadfully and disturbingly wired toward this behavior. A friend of mine calls it "hypervigilance," this state of constantly scanning the environment to prevent the next potential disaster for our children. It's survival, until it spills into the rest of my life, and I tie myself in such knots that I resemble a macramé plant holder.

I took a few extra photos of Max sitting in the seats when my son poked his head out of the car and offered a perfect sentence. "Mrs. Woods? Where do you live?"

"Right here in town," she said. Good answer, I thought. Be vague, or be followed. "But we're always around town. Anytime you see us, you can sit in our car ... if you'd like."

My son looked as if he'd just found the twin brother he'd searched for all his life. Mrs. Woods never asked about Max's disability. She never gave me the "aren't you wonderful" look, as if raising my son were a social cause rather than a love story.

We saw Mrs. Woods several more times after that first encounter. Once, as we were driving through town on Max's birthday, we saw her car parked at the post office. I turned around so abruptly that we nearly had a rollover. When I told her that it was Max's birthday, she let him play in her car for nearly an hour. It was the best gift he could have received, and to my delight, we exchanged phone numbers. As we drove away I feasted on this woman's openness and compassion toward Max. It was as if she'd spread out a big picnic blanket around her and intentionally left extra room just in case a stranger got hungry.

Mrs. Woods called one day with bad news: she was trading in her Audi. "Oh no," I gasped. "I thought Max might like to come over and see it one last time, have a chance to say goodbye," she offered. I was crushed, and we rushed over like grieving relatives.

When we arrived at her home, Max's enthusiasm for the car was contagious. He pulled Mrs. Woods and her two children into a seat-hopping frenzy. When Mr. Woods arrived home from work, Max made him squeeze into the Audi too. We looked like a circus act endlessly wedging people into a toy car until body parts poked out the windows.

Eventually, our conversation steered away from dashboards and leather seats. Mr. Woods did a double take when I told him that Max played sports — basketball, bowling, soccer — and that baseball was his favorite. "We're a baseball family," he enthused. "We love *everything* about the game." He asked me all sorts of questions: "Where does he play?" "How does it work?" "Who are the kids?"

"Max isn't able to play on a regular baseball team," I explained. "So he's on a challenger league — it's all special-needs kids — the kids who otherwise wouldn't get to play. They're so happy to be out on the field rather than watching from the sidelines. They try really hard, and the kids cheer for each other. They help each other. It's not about competition — they don't even keep score. It's just about the joy of the game, about being part of a team."

Mr. Woods looked fascinated, so I shared one of my favorite stories about the team. There's a boy named Chris, who's essentially mute. He always plays first base. When a batter gets a hit and runs toward him, Chris waits. Then, at the very last second, just as the runner is about to step on the base, Chris kicks the base to the side and the runner misses the mark. His timing is perfect. And then Chris looks over at our little group of parents watching from the bleachers and gives a huge silent laugh. He's the funniest guy I know.

One day I watched Chris pull his prank on every single player, and then Max got up to bat. The rule is that you swing until you get a hit. It must have taken Max forty tries before he slightly tapped the ball. As he was running with his knees bouncing high in the air like a parade marshal, I cringed at the thought of the base moving. But then I saw Max's foot hit squarely on the center of first base; a poof of dirt shot out from underneath. Chris hadn't moved it. Instead, I watched as Chris reached his arm around Max's shoulder and gave him a job-well-done pat on the back.

"You should come see a game sometime," I offered Mr. Woods. "It's a few towns away, but it's worth the drive. These kids are really beautiful."

"What do you mean a few towns away? Why don't we have a team like that in our town?" Mr. Woods asked.

I didn't have the answer, but he did.

WHAT I DIDN'T KNOW IS THAT Mr. Woods was on the board of the youth baseball league in our town. The very next day he approached the other board members and proposed a challenger league in our town. Max would have preferred if he'd donated his Audi to a good cause, like our driveway, but after thoughtful negotiations, the board and our town agreed to begin a challenger baseball team.

Thirty children showed up for that first game, each with a different need. Everyone had a turn swinging the bat. Some rolled in wheelchairs around the bases, and some ran the bases and never stopped running. The only thing better than watching the kids was seeing Mr. and Mrs. Woods behind the home-plate fence. The look on their faces was the same expression Max wore when he'd seen their Audi. Mr. and Mrs. Woods were handing out cups of water and juice, cheering for the kids, and tugging at the sides of their picnic blanket to make room for more.

AFTER ONE OF THE GAMES, I took Max for ice cream. People were lined up twenty deep at this popular spot. It's hard for Max to wait under the best circumstances, but as we stood near the back of the line we heard thunder. And then a few drops of rain. Max was getting visibly anxious, but so desperately did he want his strawberry sorbet that he refused to go back to the car. People were looking at us; some were smiling, most were trying to pretend that they actually meant to look past us, at a tree or a plastic cow. I kept my arms around Max and repeated to him: "We'll have ice cream — the storm won't get us — I'll keep you safe, Max."

The girl in line ahead of us eventually turned around. She looked a bit older than Max, with tiny bone structure and a face splattered with freckles. "It's okay, Max," she said assuringly, looking straight into his eyes. It was only then I realized she had some mild cognitive disabilities. Her father, who stood beside her, smiled at me with an extra dose of gentleness.

I studied her face, wondering how she knew my son. Then I realized that she didn't — she had simply overheard me talking to Max.

"You can go in front of me, Max," she offered. "I used to be scared like that too, but I'm not anymore. You can go first."

I melted a little. "Thank you. That's really nice of you," I said. She stood facing us with startling openness, a complete freedom that made her look as if she were floating several inches above the ground.

"That's something I can do," she said, shrugging her shoulders. "Come on," she beckoned, and we stepped forward to take her place in line.

CHAPTER 21

FINDING TREASURE

When my brothers and I were young, we knew, based on solid evidence, money grew on trees. We often visited our grandmother who lived in a suburb of Boston not far from our home. As our mom drove us up the long driveway that led to our grandmother's house, my brothers and I would press our noses against the car windows and pop our eyes out of their sockets like binoculars. Before the car had even come to a full stop, we'd bolt toward the two enormous pines that dwarfed her ranch-style house.

Emygram, as we called our maternal grandmother, had removed several of the lower branches of these great pines after they had broken in a storm. What remained were the sticky scars along the trunks that filled with pine pitch. And it was from these glue-like patches that money grew: pennies, nickels, dimes, even quarters.

The wonderful thing about these trees, aside from the obvious, is that money grew at all levels of the trunk. Being the youngest with two older brothers who were taller, and considerably faster, this was personally significant. Every kind of coin grew along the bottom of the tree trunks, near the grass, where I could reach. Other coins grew very high where only my oldest brother, Wendell, could reach. And in between were coins for my brother Chris.

We would bring our freshly picked coins into my grandmother's home, wash off the dirt and pine pitch, and spread our treasures across her speckled gray countertops. Her 1950s galley kitchen would bulge with excitement. "What did you *find*?" she would ask in her most surprised voice. We were certain that our grandmother, with such a resource, had more money than anyone on the planet. Until one day when we arrived early and saw that the true treasure was this sweet, loving woman, standing in her front yard, and pressing something into the scars along her trees.

Max shares this same excitement when he visits his grandparents in Florida. While he hasn't found any money trees yet, he does love the free sodas on the flights. This vacation was coming at just the right time; I needed a break from our routine. Now that Max was attending the right school, the outlook had brightened. Yet as he was getting older there was a growing "Can't Do" list the world stamped across his forehead. I could wallpaper our home with the number of evaluations that stated the limits not only autism, but also other people, now set on his life. I closed my eyes at thirty-three thousand feet, marveling at my son's ability to fly on a plane, and let the hum of the 737 muffle my thoughts.

We landed and Max bounced off the airplane, eyes bright with anticipation of his time with "Grandpa" and "Happy," my stepmother Patty's grandmother alias. The lightness in Max's steps never gave away the three diet sodas weighing down his pockets, courtesy of the kindly flight crew. Max ran toward his grandparents with a huge double-armed hug, clutching his "Florida To Do" list:

1. Visit Publix grocery store
2. See the refrigerators at CVS pharmacy
3. Drive on specific highways and take photographs of street signs, bridges, and traffic lights

The Chamber of Commerce has apparently overlooked such attractions. And no trip would be complete without a visit to Grandpa's church.

For the past several years attending church with Max had been a challenge. Max loved our home church in Massachusetts back when he was a toddler, standing on my lap during the service and bouncing to the contemporary music. He even enjoyed the classrooms as long as I went with him. But once Max turned eight, Sunday school became like every other part of his life; he just couldn't cope. I tried keeping him in the service with me, carving out a spot in the back where Max could move around and I could hear the sermon, but I couldn't keep him quiet. And once he got bored it was like trying to push the pin back into a hand grenade: it was only a matter of time before he blew. Now, with Max in his early teens, it wasn't much different. We became like so many other families I know with autistic loved ones; we stopped going to church. Or at least, I stopped bringing Max.

My dad's church setting in Florida offers an alternative. Outside the sanctuary is an oversized lobby with comfortable chairs and television monitors broadcasting the service. It's a perfect place for us: I can hear the message, and Max can be ... Max. There's even a bookstore and a place to buy coffee and ice cream and snacks. The teaching of the church is solid, but the lobby feels like it could be the cozy waiting area of a spiritual spa.

When Sunday arrived, Max and I curled into two soft chairs and agreed to meet Grandpa and Happy after the service. It's rare to find Max's off switch, but the music grabbed his attention. I slouched into the velvety chair and took a moment to breathe.

"What's that?" Max said, jolting my thoughts. "What's she doing?" he said as he stared at the television monitor.

"The lady on TV? In the church? She's being baptized," I answered. "It means ... that she loves Jesus," I explained, simplifying the situation. This woman looked as nervous as I had been when I was baptized.

Max's eyes were stuck to the TV until the woman was wrapped in a towel, the church applauded, and the music began to play. Max started bouncing as if he were at a kid's birthday party and squealed, "I want to be baptized in Grandpa's pool."

"What?"

Max was silent.

"Max!" I said leaning toward him. "Say that again?"

"I want to be baptized in Grandpa's pool," he repeated, his eyes lit with the reflection of the television monitor.

Just then my dad stepped out of the sanctuary to make sure we were all right. As he walked toward us I stared him down like a hunting dog and blurted out, "Max just told me he wants to be baptized in your pool."

We couldn't stop talking about it. "Do you think he knows what it means? Is he capable of understanding?"

We began to ask Max questions about the Bible, about faith, about Jesus. The interrogation continued for days. But Max never broke. He's a fact factory, with an answer to every question. Still, we hesitated.

Every now and then, as we'd question Max, I'd feel completely impulsive, as if I wanted to fly at this beautiful thought like a bird. For years Christian friends had told me stories about their children's faith in Jesus, and how they were being baptized as believers. I felt disconnected, listening as if it were a foreign film and I was reading subtitles. I couldn't let myself get close enough to bear our reality that this, like so many other things, could never be our life. One night, as I prayed at the end of my son's bed, I asked God to search Max's heart. "If Max doesn't have the ability to express his faith, Lord, then please choose Max as if he had. But if he is able to understand, then I pray he'll accept you, even if he's never able to voice it."

Now here stood my precious thirteen-year-old, still wide-eyed with anticipation as our skepticism flew by him like stray bullets. He was unmoved. I once told our pastor, Paul, that even though Max can't come to church anymore, he loves to memorize Scripture and read his Bible and watch his Christian videos. He's drawn to the things of God.

Paul nodded his head and said, "The Holy Spirit speaks Max's language."

Those words stayed with me. Now they were like gears clicking into place. It's not about our ability to speak or what we can and can't do; it's about our willingness to listen deep within our soul.

At the exact same moment, my dad and I realized we were making this too difficult; Max should be baptized. Now there was another problem. My dad, though a Baptist, believes only clergy should baptize, and the church then embraces the new convert. But Max couldn't possibly walk in front of the church to be baptized, and he would be too anxious if the pastor came to us. So my dad called the pastor of his church in Florida and arranged to be ordained for the day, just to baptize his grandson. And the pastor said they would welcome Max as a member of the church.

I drew pictures to help Max process what would happen during baptism and what it all meant. And I knew teaching him visually would squelch the disturbing picture lurking in my own mind of Max cannonballing into baptism. I also reminded him of the important rule pertaining to one's bathing suit.

Max knew it was different. When the time came, my son walked slowly into the water holding his grandfather's hand and calmly turned to face him. My dad reached his arm around Max, who immediately held his nose, just as he had seen the woman do at church. Max was round and soft at thirteen, and still baby-faced. As my dad spoke I breathed in this moment so still and deep; an unbroken circle of faith passed between generations. My dad, who has deeply influenced my own journey of faith, baptized my son. There were no crowds to applaud when it was over or music to play in the sanctuary. It was just Grandma Happy and me cheering from the side of the pool.

I'll admit that I looked up at the sky expecting to see the iridescent shimmer of an angel's wing, visual confirmation of this beautiful event, an ethereal high-five. I didn't see anything until I looked back down at the swirling water that surrounded my son, who was now leaping and shouting, "I got baptized!" In that glistening water

I saw every report that stamped Max insufficient, every rejection he has endured, every label the world had stuck to Max's broken places. It all washed away.

A YEAR LATER MY DEAR FRIEND SUE CALLED ME. She was organizing a day long conference and needed someone to share her personal story of faith. While praying about a speaker, she told me, my name came to her.

"Are you sure it was *my* name?" I questioned. "Maybe you should pray again. You know, best two out of three?"

She laughed but didn't budge. "And bring the baptism drawing you did for Max," she added.

I arrived early in the morning after a fitful night's sleep. I can easily talk to a crowd about autism, but talking about *me* is quite another story. I fixed the baptism drawing to the wall behind the podium, if only because I knew that subject would fill up a little airtime. Max is so happy about his baptism that every time we swim at the pool in Florida he pretends he's being baptized. Still, it didn't seem like the right audience. These were Christian women, with Christian children, in a Christian school. I think they're past the basics of baptism.

When I finished speaking, a woman approached me. "My daughter Amy is quite disabled," she shared. Yes, I thought. Let's move to the subject of autism. "For a long time Amy's been asking to be baptized. We've always told her no, because we weren't sure she understood." I stared into this woman's dark brown eyes willing her words to come forward. "But, after hearing about Max's baptism and seeing those pictures, I can't wait to go home and talk to my husband." I held my breath, as Max's private baptism, which I had neatly tucked into our spiritual scrapbook, became a bold statement of faith. Her smile took up her entire face as she said, "It's time we listened to Amy." We stared at each other for a moment, in silence, as our hearts twisted together like vines.

CHAPTER 22

LEGACY

Faith is not the only thing my dad has passed along to Max. Like hair and eye color, something else runs in our family, even though it no longer actually runs.

You see, my dad had a car. And when he was done with it, he passed it along to me. And when I was done with it, I passed it along to my niece, Stephanie, who had just learned to drive. After she drove it for a time, Max decided to claim his heritage as next in line for "Grandpa's Audi." At age sixteen Max didn't want to drive it, thankfully. He simply, desperately, wanted the seats. It's one of his passionate interests, as our friend Mrs. Woods will testify. Max can't be influenced by how others define beauty. To Max, a leather Audi seat is a magnificent work of art, the Sistine Chapel of the auto industry. While he struggles to see the big pictures of life, he has a keen ability to zoom in on the details. Fortunately, by now Max had learned to write. So he launched a letter-writing campaign.

"Dear Stephanie," he wrote, "Can I buy your Audi seat?"

"Not right now, Max," she wrote back from her room at college. "I need my seat for driving and riding." Max is so enamored with his cousin that she could have sent back her grocery list and Max would have slept with it under his pillow.

"Maybe you could use a lawn chair for driving," Max suggested in his next letter.

"No," she answered kindly. "I need my Audi seat."

"Maybe," Max would gently persuade, "the seat will fall out and then I could have it."

"No," she wrote back. "I don't think my seat will fall out."

"Maybe," Max replied, "I could use a wrench."

His correspondence began to read like something pasted together from cut-out magazine letters. Eventually, 160,000 miles and a stack of letters later, the engine quit. It was perhaps the most exciting news in Max's life. Surgery was scheduled, a team of specialists assembled, which consisted of my brother Wendell and his two daughters, and the seats were carefully removed from the car.

"Stand back, Max," I ordered, gripping Max's arm as we stood in my brother's office, the first seat now lying on a worktable. "Uncle Wendell's Inventing Room," as Max calls it, is filled with huge saws and sanders and vacuums powerful enough to make your enemies disappear. It was the perfect place to construct a chair base for the seats and create anyone's nightmare with Max.

"Okay, Max," Wendell said. "Here are your safety glasses." Max put them on and looked completely adorable. Safety glasses, I thought, what a nice touch! "Now," Wendell said, "come over here so that you can hold the saber saw."

"Whoa! Whoa!" I said as if a truck ran over my foot. "Hold the saw? Wendell! Are you kidding?"

Wendell assertively nodded his head toward Max. "You can do this, Max. I'll show you what to do." My brother stood beside Max, who looked so electrified you would have thought he was plugged in. "You have to listen, Max. I'm going to tell you the rules." Max stood as still as I've ever seen him, absorbing each word. "Now, I want you to hold the saw right here," Wendell said as he took Max's hand and placed it on the back of the saw, right beside his own. "Okay, Max. I'm turning it on," Wendell said. I felt like I was bound and gagged watching my son hold a power tool as every mother cell in my body screamed "wrong!"

They made the first cut. Max threw a glance at me through his safety glasses. He looked like he'd just come up from a brand-new underwater world with his snorkel all fogged up with excitement. "Yeah, you did it," Stephanie yelled from the side. "Good job, Max," her younger sister, Rebecca, added. Wendell stayed steady. "Good. Now, we're going to make the next cut here," he said, with their hands together on the back of the saw handle.

My brother and his daughters floated around Max like humming-birds in a garden, building together for hours. Stephanie is a little older than Max, and the source of his innocent infatuation. Rebecca is a bit younger than Max, and a good pal. These two girls have every advantage in life: the best educations, travel, the right to use a season as a verb, as in, "Where do you summer?" But with all those distractions they know how to be present with Max, to step comfortably onto his unsteady ground and smooth it out a little. I'd like to think he's given something to them in return.

Several hours later the Audi seats were done. "Sit in the driver's seat, Mom," Max ordered as he bounced on his tiptoes. I slipped into the seat and felt the cool leather on my back, just as I remember when we owned it. I thought about my dad sitting in that seat, and Steph-anie, and the threads that tie our family together. I thought about how our family has come around Max and me, just as they've done building this seat. Through all our unique and often intense needs, I've witnessed the very best in my family. "My turn, Mom!" Max yelled. He bounced into the seat with a gigantic smile and squealed, "Grandpa's seat!"

AS PERFECT AS THE GIFT OF THESE SEATS WAS, seats that have been passed down from Max's grandfather and now sit in our living room right next to the Kennedy rocker, Max has given something to his grandfather too. It's not fair to compare, but from my per-spective, Max gave the more valuable gift. It's a story that really began when I was six, but I'll start by telling you what happened when *Max* was six.

Max and I had just arrived in Florida to spend Christmas with my dad and Patty when they were both hit with the flu. Max, at six, needed full-time care; I couldn't walk away from him for a moment. So after a few days confined to bed, my dad came downstairs to join us, setting up his pillow and blanket on the couch.

Not only did Max need full supervision, he also needed to be engaged and entertained and directed. For hours at a time I played with Max, building block bridges and train tracks that sprawled across the floor. We read books and sang songs. We laughed. We sat together in soft velvety hugs. Max didn't appear to notice his grandfather on the couch, who was dozing in and out of sleep. Then again, at age six, Max didn't *appear* to notice much. Even when my dad was well, his efforts to engage and teach his grandson were awkward. Max would either walk away from his grandfather or cry.

The flu was persistent, forcing my father to stay on the couch for days. Typically, my dad has more energy than Max, always moving, thinking, going at a hundred miles an hour. He's been that way as far back as I can remember. My brothers and I love to tease him about one of his favorite expressions. When we're all on vacation together and transitioning from one scheduled activity to the next, he'll say, "Let's all take five minutes and relax." We actually had to explain to him why this is funny. Without skipping a beat he responded, with his lip slightly curled, "Six minutes of relaxation would be wasteful."

As my dad lay ill, an interesting thing started to happen. Whenever he would get up from the couch, Max would dive into his empty spot and lie down in all the warmth of where his grandfather had just been. "Max has flu," he would say, his face filled with excitement as he pulled the blanket up to his chin. "Max is Grandpa."

My dad overheard Max and me praying one night before bed. Max's prayers are awkward and rote — and beautiful. We asked God to bless our memorized list of family and friends we were thankful for. But when we were done, my dad said something that made me feel like I was a teenager again; I wanted to slam a door and walk

away. "I didn't hear you and Max pray for Garry and his new family."
I wondered if his fever was causing delirium.

I thought I was doing more than my share. I'd never said a negative word to Max about his father and only focused on the good. My mother taught me that lesson. When my brothers and I were growing up, despite my parent's divorce and all that certainly comes with that package, I never heard our mom complain or name call or label. Actually, she said wonderful things about our dad. In her selflessness, she not only left the door open for us to have a relationship with our father, but she used her own foot to wedge that door open.

My dad didn't give me any wiggle room to escape. "You need to pray for Garry," he said. "You need to pray for Garry and his new family." I didn't realize until later the power of his advice, that praying for someone else lets us see a ray of God's immense love for them, and some of that light spills back onto us.

As soon as my dad was well enough, he brought Max and me back to the airport to fly home earlier than planned, although we'd already been tick-dipped in germs. We stood together in the airport gate, heartbroken that we'd lost our precious time together. My dad still looked pale and shaky. We struggled with conversation as we both looked at Max, just six years old and sitting between us in his beloved stroller. My mind flashed back to the time when I was the one who was six. The emotions were uncomfortably familiar.

That was just about the time I started to fly to Washington to visit my dad and Patty for a week at a time. I was such a wisplike girl back then. As much as I was always anxious to get back home to Massachusetts, I'd stand in the airport, waiting to board the plane, feeling as if I'd forgotten to pack something important. My parents divorced when I was too young to have a moment of great realization; I don't remember ever throwing myself into tantrums of tears. Life bumped along. It's just that not having my dad around all the time made the world feel more spacious than it probably should have, as if everything I did had a little echo.

I was in high school when my father became a Christian. But at that point I was in the prime of my hair-and-makeup phase of life, quickly moving into my college years of limited brain-cell vacancies for anything other than me. I didn't notice how *much* he'd changed and how, in his still very busy life, he had become remarkably available.

But a few years later, before Max, I did notice the change. It was after my dad's stomach surgery. I stayed with him in his room for days on end, wiping his brow with a cool cloth and talking him out of his fever-induced hallucinations. My dad had always been so self-sufficient, so extraordinarily capable, that I never had room to step in and simply be there for him. Until then. During the day, Patty and my brothers were there too. Sometimes, as the stress and exhaustion eroded our sense of composure, we'd get punchy and start laughing because it was too hard to hold it all together. "No, Dad, Emily does not have whiskers," we'd giggle. Although after I'd spent eleven straight days sleeping in a chair beside him, he might not have been too far off.

In the middle of the night, when no one else was around, I'd sit beside his bed. The only sound was the occasional beeping of the IV and the muffled voices of the night nurses in the hall. The world felt very small in that sterile hospital room. I'd hold his hand and stare, for the first time, memorizing the tiniest details of my father's face. He would open his eyes every now and then and, comforted by my presence, close them again. The only light that would remain on at night was the florescent bulb over his bed that shone on the two of us, as if we were in a father-daughter spotlight dance.

And from that moment on our relationship changed. The bond between us grew intense, as if we both needed to make up for lost time. And when I hit my toughest struggles in life, my dad was there, loving me, comforting me, holding my hand with the same tenderness we had discovered in that hospital room.

Now, standing with my dad in the airport gate ready to bring Max back home to Massachusetts, we were struggling with the loss of our precious time together because of the flu. There just wasn't a choice but to leave Florida early, before Christmas, and head back home before Max and I both ended up ill as well. My dad and I nervously looked at our feet and scuffed our shoes against the carpeting.

Finally, my dad spoke. "I watched Max this week," he said. "He talks to you more than I knew he was able." I nodded and ran my fingers through Max's hair as he sat in his stroller. "He plays with you, Emily. I didn't know he could do so much. He's really sweet."

"I know," I said. "You just have to meet him where *he* is, join him in *his* interests."

When Max and I returned to Florida the following spring, my dad had cleared his schedule. He actually took the whole week off. At first, devoting his week to playing on Max's terms was as ill fitting as a new suit, pulling and tugging and gaping in all the wrong places. But eventually, this new style began to fit my dad. It was difficult to take Max places when he was six, so instead my dad and Patty and I spent hours together in the pool. We took Max for long walks in the stroller and repeatedly drove him over his favorite bridges. And something beautiful started to happen between Max and my dad, between all of us. As Max grew older, and we all became more able, our weeks filled with mini golf and playgrounds and walks through the zoo — and, of course, visits to every store with appliances. Sometimes we sat together without a schedule, just being.

One day, not long ago, we were all playing in the pool together. Max was in the shallow end; my dad and I were in the deep end. "Be a sea monster, Grandpa!" Max yelled in his deep teenage voice, as he threw a foam noodle toward us. My dad pulled the long noodle up to his mouth like a snout and made a sea monster noise, which I believe was very accurate. Max laughed so hard we all came unglued. "Do it again, Grandpa!" Max laughed as he shot out of the water like a geyser. This isn't the way others get to see my dad; it's reserved for Max, something beautiful unlocked by a grandson with autism. And it's the side that lets me be six again with my dad — for the very first time.

CHAPTER 23

DANCING AT
THE BACK DOOR

"Don't get out, Max. It's not time yet," I ordered as we sat in our car, watching the front door of the church. Services are no longer held in the rented warehouse building as they were when Max was a toddler. Now they're held in a handsome new building, one that our church owns.

"You're gonna love this, Max," I tried to convince him. I knew there was *one* thing my son loved about the service at our church: he loved it to be over. He can't stand the sermon or "the talking," as he tells me. It's not an issue of theology, exactly; Max is paralyzed with fear when someone's voice booms through a microphone, and he can't follow the concepts. But expecting our pastor to either skip the sermon or build a megalobby with television monitors like my dad's church seemed a bit of a stretch.

This *has* to be better than the last time I tried bringing Max to church, I thought, when he stood outside the sanctuary and screamed through the entire service. I couldn't even get him to leave. That was a year ago, and the memory was making my stomach churn. Everyone understood; people at this church loved seeing Max when he used to come with me, before it became impossible for him to sit quietly through a service, before his needs became too great for him to cope with a classroom. They'd gotten used to seeing me come to church alone whenever Max was enjoying a weekend with his father, but it felt wrong. Max belongs in church. We belong in church together. Max was even baptized now. Everyone who enters this sanctuary, *any* sanctuary, is scared and messy with a history of failures; it's just that only some of us show it on the outside too.

Finally, I saw someone walking through the door of the church and knew this was, perhaps, the craziest thing I'd ever felt compelled to do with my son. "Okay, Max," I said boldly opening my car door. "It's time. Let's go in."

As soon as we entered, Max broke loose from my hand and darted straight into the sanctuary, dodging and weaving through people like a linebacker. "Emily!" a friend called. "What are you doing? You missed church. It's over." Before I could explain, the crowd pulled my friend away. I stood there, trying to see where Max had gone and wishing I'd taped one of those tall orange bicycle flags to his back.

"Did someone forget to set their alarm clock today?" my friend Jean teased as he walked toward me with his wife, Ayn.

"No, we were *trying* to miss church," I answered. Jean laughed and gave me an exaggerated nod. "No, really," I insisted. "Max is with me." I looked into the church, trying to find evidence of his bright striped shirt but still couldn't see him, so I turned back to Jean and Ayn, ready to plead my insanity defense. "I want Max to come to church again, and he always did well at the end when everyone's milling around and talking. So we just … showed up for the end," I laughed. "We're calling it backwards church."

Jean, also a designer, was used to creative thinking. "Backwards church?" he questioned. A few other friends were gathering around me. I suddenly felt self-conscious about this idea, as if people might be wondering if I'd finally crossed the line from a fairly normal artist to someone who might potentially cut my own ear off.

"Well … I thought we'd start with where Max has been success-ful," I explained. "You know, build on his strengths. If it works, we'll come a little earlier each time. Who knows, maybe someday Max will sit through the sermon."

I looked back, searching for Max. With the church now clearing out, I could see him jumping up and down in the middle of the sanctuary where other kids were throwing a foam football and leaping off the stage. He fit in beautifully. So I took a deep breath and turned back to talk with my friends for a few minutes. And then I caught a glimpse of Max.

"Oh, no," I cringed as I saw Max lifting a chair up over his head. I lunged toward Max. "He's okay, Emily," Jean called behind me, but before I could get to Max another friend intercepted. She grabbed my shoulders and gave me a hug. I looked past her and could see several men from church now handling the situation with Max, pointing to where the chair belonged. Relax, I reminded myself. This is working.

The church felt cavernous now that it was almost void of people. I stood beside Max, his cheeks flushed from all the excitement as we prepared to leave. One of the men who had helped with the chair incident walked up to Max. He looked him straight in the eyes and lovingly placed his hand on Max's shoulder. "Thanks for the help stacking chairs with us today, Max. We could use your help again."

Max didn't say a word, but stood still, listening.

"We'd like to make you an official member of our team: the Grunt Crew," Jeff said, with his hand still on Max's shoulder as if my son were being knighted.

"What's Grunt Crew?" I asked, feeling like I'd missed a few chapters in a book.

"Would you like that Max? Would you help us?" Jeff asked again without breaking his gaze.

Max's back straightened and, wide-eyed, he turned to me. He sucked in a huge gasp of air and held his breath as if waiting for my approval. I didn't really know what they were talking about, but the atmosphere was electrified. I burst into a smile and nodded.

Max turned back to Jeff and bounced straight up on his toes. "Yes," he said breathlessly. "Yes."

MAX RAN INTO THE CHURCH ON TIPTOES, as if there were angels holding him under each arm and dangling him down toward the earth, while he held on to his heavenly Hoover vacuum. Max was right on time for being late. He'd become a regular, serving on the Grunt Crew for a year or so now, even adding vacuuming to his repertoire of service. It was the highlight of his week, stacking the chairs so that the youth group could use the open space during the week.

Max stacked several chairs that morning, lifting them onto a cart as if they were weightless. And then he stopped to soak it all in, looked around at the ten or so men working beside him, and threw his hand into the air. With a huge thumbs-up sign Max yelled, "Now that's teamwork!" His smile filled the entire sanctuary.

"One, two, three, four, watch Max do a lot more," Jean said, prompting Max to stay on task.

Max started back to his job, running between chairs and dropping each one on top of the stack with all the fanfare of a magic trick. Poof, the chair is gone. Ta-da, it's on the stack. And then Max called out his own rhyme, "We need you, on the Grunt Crew." I watched the other men as they peeked at Max out of the corners of their eyes, smiling.

"We should all be that happy," a woman said to me as she walked by.

"I know," I said with my heart exploding. "Fortunately, he doesn't know how to contain his emotions."

One of the deacons came up beside me, his arms folded across his chest as we watched Max. "If our congregation had just 10 percent of Max's joy and enthusiasm for service," he said, "it would transform our church, any church for that matter."

That was right about the time my dear friend Sue began calling Max "the Joy Boy" — and for good reason. His freshness draws people in, startles them. It's irresistible.

Someone else was watching Max's joy that morning, a guest speaker at our church. I'm sure he was wonderful, had I actually gone to church to hear him. After the service he was standing in the sanctuary and talking with Paul, our pastor, when he pointed to Max. "Tell me about this boy," he said to Paul. "What's his story?"

"That's Max," Paul answered and explained his role on the Grunt Crew, and that Max comes not for the service but to serve. The guest speaker was intrigued, so Paul asked if he'd heard Chuck Colson talk about his autistic grandson on the radio.

Indeed, this man had. "I don't agree with everything Chuck Colson says," the man answered, "unless he's talking about his grandson. That's our common ground."

Paul smiled as he looked back at Max and said, "This *is* Chuck Colson's grandson."

The guest speaker's eyes welled with tears, and he walked out of the church to return home where, as we would later discover, his own young son with autism was waiting.

MAX HAS NEVER SAT THROUGH A SERMON AT OUR CHURCH — at least not yet. I've taken it off our immediate list of goals. God has a mission for Max at our church, backward as it may once have appeared. Max doesn't just come to church; he's part of the church. And he is loved. But we do come earlier now for Grunt Crew so that Max can hear the music at the end of the service. He arrives in time to throw the doors open and stand with me in the back doorway as he holds his as-seen-on-TV Swivel Sweeper in one hand, like a shepherd with a staff. The lights are down and the words appear on a screen behind the musicians. Max can read well and points to words he especially likes, spells them aloud, even sings a little. And when the congregation is really fortunate, he dances. Max's joy of worship is so pure and free that it feels as though someone sprayed air freshener all around us.

As Paul says, "Church isn't over until Max dances at the back door."

One Sunday, with Max in his midteens, we were standing together in the open doorway, listening to the music and holding hands. He was so excited that he was bouncing on his toes, and I started bouncing too. I felt such gratitude that it was practically narcotic. And then the music team began to play a song called "I Can Do All Things," using the Scripture from Philippians 4:13: "I can do all things through Christ who gives me strength."* It reminded me of the Superman symbol I'd drawn in the margin of my Bible. Apparently, the song reminded Max of a video he loves by the Donut Man. First Max was just pointing to the words on the screen. Then, he started doing what appeared to be the cha-cha. But when it came to the refrain, Max couldn't hold back.

"I can do all things ...," the congregation sang with the music team. There was meant to be a silent pause, but Max filled it, his voice slicing through the darkness of the church.

"How many things?" Max yelled from the back of the sanctuary as he lunged into the service with his fist in the air.

"I can do all things," the church answered in song.

"A million things?" Max asked the congregation.

And they answered, "I can do *all* things through Christ who strengthens me."

---

*This song was written by David Coate, our church's worship pastor, from his new CD, *The New Hymn Project*, newhymnproject.com.

CHAPTER 24

UNSPOKEN GRACE

"Max, can you stop talking for just a minute? I can't hear myself think."

Yes, I actually said these words, this parental right of passage, to my teenage son as we were getting ready to go to bowling. I didn't mean it *really*. I was just trying it on for size. Plus, I start to come unglued around the third hour of talking about commercial refrigerators.

"Until?" he asked.

"How about quiet from 4:00 until 4:10?" I suggested.

"How about ..." Max studied his digital watch. "... until 4:05."

"Okay, Max. Quiet until 4:05."

"And then?" he asked.

"And then we'll talk some more about refrigerators, and it will be time for bowling."

"And what's after bowling?" he asked.

"And then we'll go out to dinner with your friends."

"And what's after dinner with your friends?"

Max can go on like this until I've given him the schedule for the next millennium, which shoots the whole idea of a few minutes of quiet. But I don't mind. Truthfully, I savor every word. While Max has made great strides, we still have horrifying moments when I watch my son open his mouth as if he were choking, searching for a word he knows, while only pushing silence into the room. I can only imagine how frustrating it has been for him over the years, as if words catch in his mind like the thread of a sweater, pulling his thoughts into a tangled mess. We've learned to rely on unspoken language: pictures, written lists, gestures, and our Picture Talks. Being still and listening is essential; sometimes words just get in the way.

But all this makes it difficult to make friends, which is why we joined this special-needs bowling league: friendship and because, as our friend Sue says, we take fun seriously.

We arrived at bowling and were greeted by Max's team members, Evan and Brendan, along with their mothers. Evan was first to bowl with his usual dramatic flair. He's a little older than Max, with Down syndrome, and looks like he's just popped out of the 1950s with a monogrammed bowling shirt and crew cut. We cheered for him as he bowled a good frame. Thrilled with his success, Evan yelled, "Scooby Do!" and rubbed his hands together like he was about to eat a piece of chocolate cake.

Brendan, a handsome young man in his early twenties, was next. He's not as agile. His mother held one arm, and an assistant held the other, steadying Brendan as he walked into position. He uses a ramp to bowl, an aluminum structure that works like a slide, allowing him to simply tap the ball to make it roll toward the pins. As soon as Brendan gave the ball a push he turned away and never saw that it knocked down every pin. We call that his poker face.

Max was up next, bouncing and skipping into position like Tigger. Even Baryshnikov couldn't make 170 pounds look so light. He took aim and carefully rolled the first ball straight down the gutter, because it's as interesting as knocking down the pins. And when he didn't think we were looking, he pulled his favorite move and rolled two balls at once. I would laugh more than I'd correct him. But don't get the wrong idea. Just like my own mom, I do insist on some stringent rules, like "The heater vents in our home may no longer be used as a depository for Mom's credit cards," and "Pants are not optional." And when it comes to bowling, "Balls must be aimed toward the pins, not the spectators." So far, Max has been able to follow this rule most of the time, and I've been agile enough to intervene before he becomes a local news story.

Part of the thrill of bowling is dinner after the game at a local sandwich shop. With our boys, dinner is also classified as an extreme sport, with ketchup shooting through the air, ham and cheese bouncing out of sandwiches, and potato chip bags crackling like a cheering crowd. When our food arrived at our very first dinner together, everyone dove in except Max. He just held out his hands, waiting, without saying a word.

My mind raced.

Of course it was Max's routine to pray before dinner, but I hadn't planned on praying with these families. We didn't know them that well yet or understand where they stood on issues of faith. People are used to grabbing hands to pray before meals in the Bible Belt, but this is New England, where drivers use dirty looks instead of directional signals and smiling at a stranger can be interpreted as an act of aggression. Praying with strangers doesn't always evoke the warm fuzzies. But Max doesn't understand that.

I stared at my son's sweet hand reaching for mine and I had a choice: deal with my own discomfort or forever scar my child by refusing his hand. In slow motion I captured the image of his soft velvet skin and the powerful silence hovering around my fifteen-year-old son's invitation to pray. It was the same powerful silence I remembered from church recently, the same outstretched hand of another fifteen-year-old sitting right beside me in the sanctuary. And that child, a young girl, was just as vulnerable as Max.

I remembered the way her crisp white-cotton sundress fell loosely around her tiny frame, her hands that slumped into her lap like weights. As the music in the church began, a friend leaned over my shoulder. "You should know," she whispered so close that I could feel her lips move against my ear. "The girl who just sat beside you tried to take her own life this past week." I never turned around, but I could feel the breeze of my friend rushing off and disappearing into the wings of the church, leaving me alone.

Our pastor began speaking, although I couldn't focus on a word he said. My mind was spinning like a pinwheel, praying for this young girl. All I could understand was the visual: ushers were bringing forward trays of grape juice and plates of crackers. In our seeker-friendly church, we don't typically offer Communion on Sunday mornings. This day was the exception.

I watched the silver tray of broken wafers pass along the aisle in front of me. Some pieces were large and inviting while others were so small they were nearly dust. When the tray came to our aisle, the girl in the white cotton dress passed the plate to me without taking anything, not even a crumb. Certainly she has a right to refuse. I just couldn't help but think that she had wanted to die, yet was refusing the life that died for her.

I took the plate and held it back out to her in an offering gesture. She looked down shaking her head no. Quick, think of something brilliant to say, I ordered myself. I can't take Communion and make her feel even more separate and alone. She probably thinks I don't understand. I looked down at that plate of crackers, all broken and crumbled just as I've been, just as this girl is, and had a thought. It was a brilliant thought, which is why I am certain it was not actually *my* thought. I reached in and carefully chose a cracker before passing the plate to the next person. With a crisp snap, I broke my cracker in two, and invited the girl to share in mine. I held out my hand and waited, without speaking a word. Finally, she lifted up her heavy hand to mine and took the bread of life. And she let herself smile.

Now, here I was, looking at my son's hand reaching out to me, his silent invitation to pray, as we sat with his bowling team in the middle of the sandwich shop. I had to do what that girl had done in church, to listen with my soul, to trust that I was grabbing on to something solid. I lifted my hand to Max's and let our fingers slip softly together. But it wasn't enough for Max.

"Oh! Wait," he said, looking around the dinner table at everyone else, fully expecting them to join in. They were already eating their ham-and-cheese subs. Slices of pizza were pointing into their open mouths like arrows. Suddenly, my choice felt simple. I leaned toward the others on the bowling team and invited them to join hands while we prayed. Max prayed his memorized prayer, and as always, I finished. Hands around the table released with the precision of a synchronized swim team, and no one said a word. Slowly the clicking of plastic utensils and sound of metal juice caps popping their vacuum seals invaded the silence.

The next week, after we survived another death-defying adventure in bowling, we were back at our favorite sandwich shop. As we stood at the counter ordering, Evan started to tug on his mother's sleeve. "Hands, Mommy," he pleaded. "Hands." She didn't know what he was talking about, so he tugged on her again and pointed to me. "Hands," he repeated. It took us a while, but we finally realized that in his struggle with language he just didn't know the words. He wanted to pray. I felt affirmed, like I just got the Good Housekeeping Seal of Approval. As we reached around the table creating our circle, Evan pulled his hands away just long enough to rub them together with that same chocolate-cake-in-front-of-him gesture.

The following week I was ready. I knew what "hands" meant. Oddly enough, Evan came prepared too — he had a prayer request. How did he even know to do that? He wanted us to pray about his friends' coming to visit. And then the next week, he had another request. Over the next few weeks ideas started popping out of Evan with such urgency you would have thought someone was poking him in the ribs. Some days we had to put our sandwiches down four or five times during the meal to hold hands and pray. Brendan, who doesn't have any spoken language, would laugh with the rest of us. Our prayers were far from standard and predictable. Instead, they were filled with life, perfectly imperfect, often spoken with mouths already filled with food.

Now each week after bowling we sit in the same sandwich shop together, in the same booth, and share a meal as friends. Max is still the first to hold out his hands to pray, but we all quickly follow. And each week prayer is an open conversation, as if Jesus were sitting at the table with us, completing our circle of communion, and holding ketchup-covered hands.

CHAPTER 25

THE BRIDGE

Now that my son is 170 pounds — and I'm not — there is only one thing strong enough to pull him out of bed in the morning. He hides under his blanket, slowly emerges as a hunchback, and is finally upright by the time he reaches the bathroom. But no matter how painful, Max makes sure he's downstairs on time. Max's wake-up call, by his choice, is "prayer TV."

At first it made me laugh to see Max fixated on the Catholic channel, EWTN. After all, church had been as much of a struggle as any other part of his life. And then there is the tiny detail that we're Evangelical Christians, not Catholics. Clearly Max doesn't understand that there are different denominations. But over time I grew to appreciate my son's love for his favorite morning program called *The Chaplet of The Divine Mercy*, a prayer set to song and filmed inside a beautiful chapel. With Max's impressive memory, he immediately memorized the words and sang along, even mimicking a parishioner's cough midway through. He was comforted by the repetition and predictability of the service, but he also loved that they were praying to Jesus, the common denominator of all Christian denominations. Although we were swaying to the music, we weren't swaying in our convictions. Still, some of our friends were upset that I was supporting Max's love of a Catholic intercessory prayer. You would have thought I was sitting my kid in front of an R-rated movie every morning and lighting his cigar.

When Christmas approached, I called the number displayed with the credits after every service, and I ordered a copy of the program. Max was thrilled with his gift. As I studied the back of the package, I noticed the address of the church. "Max!" I exploded. "This church is in Massachusetts!" He looked up from his Audi seat in the middle of our living room, stared at me with big, round saucer eyes like Little Orphan Annie, and shrieked, "Let's go there!"

With all our practice Max could go just about anywhere with me, as long as I had help. We even went to New York City once. It was my brother Wendell's idea; he knew Max's love for bridges, so he drove us there, over every bridge in the city. Wendell is much more daring than I and thought Max's idea of riding the New York subway was brilliant. We did it — the memory still gives me post-traumatic stress disorder. But I loved walking across the Brooklyn Bridge together, right through the clouds, as if we were part of that floating stone and steel structure that carries you from one place to another, over the obstacle in your path.

Knowing Max's challenging history with church services, I thought it best to contact this church first and find out how we could visit without being a disturbance. I explained how Max wouldn't even head off to school until after the televised service had finished. And I told them the catch — that Max has special needs, struggles with anxiety, and wouldn't do well with the service. I hoped we could just take a tour of the church when it was empty. Their response was so welcoming and exuberant that I finally had to fess up. "We're not actually ... Catholic," I timidly admitted on the phone. "We're Evangelical Christians." Apparently, it didn't matter a bit.

I recruited my mom, who's always up for adventure, to come with us as an extra pair of hands. Max adores his "Granny Nanny" and was thrilled to have a slumber party at her house the night before. Mom has never wavered from that put-a-trampoline-in-your-living-room spirit I grew up with. When Max was rinsing his dinner plate under the kitchen faucet and creating a monsoon on her countertop, my mother leaned into me with a whisper and said, "Isn't it great that he's doing so much on his own now?" There is always dancing at slumber parties, with Max pounding his feet so hard that it shakes the slab foundation of her ranch-style home, the same house that years ago had money trees growing in the front yard. My mom will smile and laugh and, wise woman that she is, move out of his way. This night before our trip was no exception. She watched Max dancing, this gargantuan teenage boy who isn't the least bit mindful of his image, and she mused, "He's wonderful, isn't he? It restores my faith in humanity."

The next morning we drove across the state to Stockbridge, Massachusetts, a charming town in the Berkshires, surrounded by rolling hills dotted with wooden barns and antique shops. Max was so excited that he could barely speak the entire three-hour trip along his favorite highway. Max has a startling ability to memorize every street sign, mileage marker, the name of each bridge we cross or pass under, and the date when it was built. When we finally arrived at the church, with our human GPS riding in the backseat, we were received as warmly as we were by phone. Carol, who would take us on a tour, walked us toward the chapel. We climbed the granite steps and pulled open the huge oak door just in time to see a horrifying sight: the back of the priest's robe floating toward the altar in a church filled with people. Please tell me I'm hallucinating, I thought. I just drove 150 miles so that my son can scream through a church service?

Just then the doors closed behind us with an echoing thud. We stood in the darkened entryway that leads to the sanctuary. As Carol started into the crowded church, Max froze.

"I don't think this is a good idea, Carol," I called in a whisper, clinging to Max's shoulders. "I don't think he'll be able to go inside."

Carol turned around and walked back toward us. "It'll be fine," she assured me. "We always close these outside doors," she said as she pushed them back open. "But today, we'll just leave them open if it's easier for Max."

Max stood in the open doorway of this beautiful chapel and watched as the service began. The music echoed against the brilliantly colored frescoes and gilded wood. Behind the altar hung a large portrait of Jesus with rays of red and white, blood and water, streaming from his heart. The service wasn't exactly as Max knew it from television, but it was close enough to hold his attention. Given his history, it was amazing that Max was even near the live service. I kept reminding him to use a quiet voice as he cowered in the dark wooden entryway, reading along with the words of the service printed in a bulletin.

Midway through, the parishioners began filing into a line in the center aisle. This wasn't on television. Suddenly, Max bolted toward the line. I jumped after him and, looking back at Carol, mouthed the words, "Is this okay?" She shook her head yes. It didn't feel okay. I knew we were the only non-Catholics in line, and for what? I felt like all those painted portraits on the walls and ceiling were watching us, their eyes following our every move like the *Mona Lisa*. I had this nervous fake smile glued on my face. But Max walked toward the priest as if he were leaping barefoot through a field, cupping his hands to catch butterflies. Someone else's butterflies, that is. On someone else's field.

Finally, Max stood alone before the priest. I watched him from behind. His expectant childlike faith was so beautiful, so willing and trusting. He didn't even know what was going to happen. The priest held up a relic of St. Faustina, a Polish mystic who, Catholics believe, received a revelation of the chaplet. The idea, as I could tell from watching others, was to kiss the relic that was set in a cross. Max must have been watching too, because before I could stop him he leaned forward and innocently put his nose on it. I think he thought people were smelling it. When he lifted his head a smile burst from the inside out. I had to almost run after him as he skipped back to the open doorway.

We watched the rest of the service from there. When the priest finished, I looked at my mom and let out a sigh. "We did it." But

I was wrong; it wasn't quite over. My son noticed that the service didn't end exactly the way it does on television, which I'm sure in his mind was a glaring omission. So, from the back of the church, in a very unquiet voice, Max assisted the priest by finishing the service properly. "Copyright EWTN!" he yelled. "To order this or other religious broadcasts, contact …," and then gave the address, telephone number, and website. It was one of those perfect Max moments. I plastered my hands over my mouth trying to stifle my laughter.

Now that the service was *truly* over, Max bolted into the sanctuary. I had told him earlier that the church might have a little Grunt Crew work for him to do. As we walked forward we stood beside a group of nuns draped in sapphire blue habits. My eyes met with the nun closest to Max as she stretched her hand out. She was tiny and I could understand why she might be afraid that Max would bump into her. I pulled Max closer to me and smiled for her reassurance. But then another nun reached her hand up with the same gesture and briefly touched Max's shoulder. And another nun brushed his hand. They began hovering around him, each taking a turn to bless him, swooping toward him, and waving their billowing sleeves like a flock of bluebirds searching for a place to light.

ONE YEAR LATER, MAX AND MY MOM AND I were on our way back to Stockbridge for another visit. This time Carol greeted us as warmly as family. As she walked us up the stone steps toward the chapel and braced the doors open, she burst into a smile. "Everyone knows Max is coming," she giggled with the excitement of a little girl. "And today they're going to sing the service exactly as they do on television, just for Max."

My eyes welled up as we took our positions in the doorway. But Max started walking forward, right into the church. He didn't even look nervous. So I followed his lead, signaling for my mom to follow, and pointed to one of the empty pews. He sat down. He grabbed the back of the pew in front of him as if he were strapping in for a roller-coaster ride. Max's eyes darted around the ceiling and walls with this sort of Stevie Wonder head roll, soaking in the familiar beauty of the church, with its doors still open behind us.

We watched the priest walk up the aisle, and the music began. I sat on the edge of the slippery wooden pew ready to jump up and chase Max, who would certainly bolt out of the sanctuary like a wild mustang. But he didn't. Instead, he began to sing. Loudly. He was terribly off-key. And it was beautiful. He wasn't wondering if he looked right, sounded good, met the rules, or even if he were trespassing. He wasn't carrying around all the layers of heavy armor that most of us wear, the barriers that make it so hard for us to see the one thing we all hope to find in church. It's lovely to be with someone who sees Jesus more than they see our differences. It's the way I hope people see my son too.

Max bounced up and down on the wooden pew, laughing with excitement, and I couldn't help but bounce right with him. Everyone in front of us turned around, looked at Max, and smiled. I couldn't take my eyes off of him, except to look back at Carol, who now stood alone in the open doorway watching us.

When the service was over — and Max had, of course, added the credits — we walked through the open doors and into the brilliant July sun. A warm breeze fluttered our cotton clothing as our eyes met the endless landscape of rolling green hills below the chapel. We stood there exhilarated, soaking in the breathtaking beauty. I noticed a woman watching us. When I smiled back, she walked toward us. She was wearing a large wooden cross around her neck and an ankle-length denim jumper. I couldn't tell if she was a casual nun or just an earthy-crunchy-Berkshire-type.

"I'm Janice," she said. "I saw the two of you in the service."

"You did?" I blurted out excitedly.

"Yes," she nodded, looking up at Max's face.

"This is Max, my son," I said grabbing his shoulders. "He watches this on TV every day. I can't believe he sat through the whole service.

Did you hear him singing?" I was giddy with laughter. "And we're not even Catholic!"

"I have to tell you," she said. Her quiet presence startled me. "I came to church today … facing a problem. A *huge* problem. But then I saw your son's *joy*, and your joy for him." She looked down and began to smile softly. "It changed everything. It changed *me*." Now I recognized her. She was one of the people who had turned around several times in church to smile at Max. "I don't think you know," she said staring deeply into my eyes. "Max is a messenger for Jesus."

I studied this woman's face hoping to find her brilliantly discerning. It was such an incredibly powerful statement that I desperately wanted to believe her. I wanted to spread her words as a soothing salve on my own wounds for Max's circumstances.

I reached my arms around Max and didn't know how to respond. After all, this was *my Max* she was talking about, the same child who requires help and supervision 24/7, who can't attend a regular school or cross a street alone. And yet, I know what she saw in Max. I've seen it too, many times — Max connecting us to the things in life that matter on the deepest soul level. Maybe what Janice meant is that these soul-stirring moments can move us past our differences, past our obstacles, like a bridge.

Standing in the warm sun on the steps of the chapel, I closed my eyes for a moment and thought back to one particularly horrible day when my son was only six years old. And I started to laugh. It was the day when I sat in a meeting with his classroom supervisor. I watched as the supervisor rolled his eyes and spoke as if he'd never seen a child as unfortunately disabled as my son. And then he smirked as if it were pointless to help Max, a waste of time and resources. Perhaps I should have responded with kindness and offered to do something nice for him, like remove the brakes from his car. But I did the next nicest thing I could do for this man — I told him the truth. "Max is going to design bridges someday," I said as I poked my finger insistently toward him. "You just watch."

CHAPTER 26

JUMPING OFF THE BRIDGE

Look at this, Max," I said, pulling over to the side of the road just before we crossed an arched stone bridge that spanned a small inlet of water on our way to the beach. "Look what these kids are doing."

We watched through our car windshield as two boys climbed over the low railing of the bridge. Without hesitation they leapt into the air before plummeting toward the water. Lena was in the car with us too, nine years and counting now, and the three of us started to laugh. Before the boys had even emerged from the water, several more kids climbed into position.

"Mom, let's see this," Max squealed from the back seat.

"Yeah, Max," I said. "Let's see what's gonna happen." Just then the boys flew into the air waving their arms in circles to keep their balance and disappeared into the water. "Max, can I tell you something funny?"

"Yes — yes," he answered with his eyes fixed on the little lemmings.

"Mom did that once, Max. I jumped off that bridge."

It had been years earlier, when Max was young and I felt like I had a thousand pounds strapped to my back. It was on a dare with a friend, a completely impulsive moment. I hate heights, hate sharks, although the chance of there being a man-eater in this shallow bay was nil. I didn't think the bridge was high, until I climbed over the railing and stood on the other side, my bare feet balancing on a thin

ledge of stone. I felt so frightened and vulnerable standing there
with the wind blowing against me, which is why there was only one
solution.

I jumped.

And in that moment when my feet left the bridge, before they
plunged into the icy water, there was complete and total abandon-
ment. Predictability was gone. Everything emptied from my mind. I
was flying. I was free. And then I slammed back down to earth and
under the green water. I didn't know which way was up, which way
to swim. Just when I didn't think I could hold my breath any longer,
I found the surface. Gasping for air, and reassembling all the missing
parts of my bathing suit, I let out a victory cry.

"Mom. Look at this," Max said as we watched five boys position
themselves along the ledge of the bridge. At the exact same moment,
they all jumped.

"Woo-hoo, Max! That was great!"

But there was one boy who wasn't jumping. He stood on the bridge
staring at us the entire time. I assumed he thought I was someone's
parent ready to intervene. He was such a handsome kid, probably
about twelve years old, and sporting long surfer trunks over his wiry
build. He had a thick swash of sun-bleached hair that flipped away
from his forehead with the breeze. No doubt he was just a few years
away from being the heartthrob of the high school, on the conveyor
belt to Ivy League, full athletic scholarship in hand. Our postcard-
perfect town has a way of turning out kids like this, the kind of child
everyone imagines when their bellies are bulging with a baby, children who are born into privilege. If it weren't for autism, Max might
have been that kid, riding his bike down to the bay and knowing the
feeling of freedom as his feet left the bridge.

We watched a few more kids jump, and since this boy kept staring
at us, we decided it was time to head out to the beach. As we started
to drive over the bridge, this future prom king stared into our backseat and looked right at Max. And in his ear-piercing prepubescent

voice screamed to his friends and right into Max's open window, "It's the retard! I *told* you guys I was right. It *is* the retard."

We drove along the thin peninsula of land, toward the open stretch of beach in silence.

The sky was a wash of blue with subtle streaks of lavender slicing overhead like skywriting. The beach was empty except for a few people walking their dogs. We set up our blanket and cooler on our favorite dinner spot, and Max immediately opened his CD player. Most of his CDs are scratched now from bringing them to the beach, but it's well worth it. I felt like I couldn't quite swallow any food yet, so while Lena sat with Max I walked toward the water to let the cold surf wash over my feet.

With each step my feet sank into the soft sand, and I thought about all the history buried here. This is where I brought Max when I was first alone, holding my baby in my arms and singing. This is where I stood with a circle of friends and threw a cloud of Peppermint Patti's ashes into the surf. And it was on this same stretch of shore that I watched my son learn to kayak. He looked so vulnerable, floating alone on a thin sliver of a boat like a leaf on the ocean. I didn't think I could bear it. But whenever he stopped paddling and fell behind, a bright yellow tether line popped up from the sea reminding me that, even when I couldn't see it, he was still attached to his teacher's boat. That line wouldn't let him drift, and when Max didn't have the strength to row, he was pulled.

I met a woman here on this beach early this spring. She must have been in her eighties, all bundled up in a parka with the hood tied around her chin. The little circle of face that showed her skin was a "road map," as my grandmother used to say. I followed her, assuming she would need a hand over the sand dune. But before I could get to her, she picked up speed and started to run, her spindly legs and spongy white sneakers kicking up a spray of sand.

When I finally made it across the dune, I found her gazing at the ocean and holding a weathered fence post as if it were the mast of a sailboat.

"That was quite a sprint you did on that soft sand," I said, huffing and puffing. She smiled, but didn't respond. So I clarified, "That sand is hard to get through."

She laughed. "It's easier to get through the tough stuff if I give it a little muscle."

I looked at her out of the corner of my eye and said coyly, "I think there's a life lesson there."

"Nah," she refuted. "I've exercised my whole life. Lots of practice. It comes naturally now."

Like I said.

I stood there on the beach staring into the blue, trying to understand what my muscles were feeling and why they were not sore. It's not that unkind remarks don't hurt Max; they do. Terribly. But the r-word the boy spat into his window isn't part of Max's vocabulary; even now, as a young man, I knew he didn't understand. Max has made enormous progress. He has a delightful sense of humor and is able to cope with so much of life now. Max is an idea man, always armed with places he wants to see, things he wants to try. He tells me his deepest thoughts through our Picture Talks. And Max and his father have a loving relationship, one that belongs to the two of them. Max still has so much learning to do. But of all the things I hope Max will continue to learn, I pray that the cruel judgments we pass on one another will not be one of them.

I thought about that boy posing on the bridge like an Abercrombie and Fitch model, with every advantage at his fingertips, all that external beauty draped around unfinished business. Even when he jumps from a bridge, his feet are still stuck to this world. And for the first time, I knew Max and I could slip out of our hazmat suits, move unencumbered, breathe deeply. The poison hadn't touched us. Someday this boy might work as a clerk at a convenience store or wait tables at an Australian steak house for extra spending money or take his grandkids bowling. Someday he might be a classroom supervisor. I hope, for his own sake, he gets a Max in his life before then.

The beach was huge and expansive, with enough mist in the air to blend the sky and sea into one. The rolling surf played surround-sound static, and the air smelled washed clean. I was a tiny speck on that six-mile streak of sand, floating, swallowed up in a borderless watercolor painting. It's one of my favorite places to be, standing on the edge of the earth where land becomes water and water becomes sky, where one thing changes into another. I stared into the vast blue and wondered what it will be like when God lowers his rescue basket, lifts us from this place, and we are free.

The wind tapped me on the shoulder and I turned around.

There, at the top of the beach, was Max. The late afternoon sun was drenching him in a film of golden light like Easter cellophane. And he was dancing. His feet barely touched the sand. His arms and legs flew around him like a marionette that has broken free of its strings. And Lena faithfully sat beside him on the blanket. I was too far away to hear the music, but I had faith that it was playing because I could see the evidence in my son's joyful steps, my luminous little skylight boy all grown up.

A soft wind wrapped around me, as if the very breath of God was covering us with a layer of love so impenetrable that even the harshest judgments couldn't touch us, like Holy Spirit Teflon. And I remembered a voice. It was a beautiful, melodic voice — crème brûlée with a Canadian accent. It was my friend Peppermint Patti's voice, her words alive and dancing in the sand. "God works through these children. Max is a gift. These children are a gift."

There is no ordinary day in our lives, Max and me.

Sometimes there is only one thing you can do, only one thing you *should* do. And I don't want to miss that open window. So right now, I'm going to dance with my son.

LEARNING TO LOVE

CHARLES W. COLSON

This is a love story. Love is the mark of the Christian, as Francis Schaeffer once wrote, the first Christian virtue. The essence of God himself. Emily and Max have taught me about love in a deeper way than I've ever understood before. I have witnessed love that perseveres. I have marveled at how God has poured his grace through them, guiding them through agonizing trials and pain — and then I have witnessed in the end the triumph of love. For me, it has been life-changing in so many ways — and inspires us all.

Not that this has been easy. Many years ago, at the end of a wonderful family vacation, Emily and I stood beside Max's crib. We watched him, just eighteen months old, sleeping peacefully. He was the most beautiful child I'd ever seen. My first thought was what if Emily and Patty had not worked so selflessly to nurse me to health in the Georgetown Hospital? I might not have lived to see this gift.

I turned to Emily, grabbed her in an embrace, and told her how grateful I was to her and to God that I could have this moment. Both of us were struggling to hold back tears, in my case because I knew, even before the official diagnosis, that Emily was likely to raise a son with developmental challenges — and to do so alone. The very thought that my sweet, beautiful daughter would have to be brave and strong was painful. Fathers never stop feeling protective of their daughters, no matter how old they are. Could she do it, I wondered?

There were many trying moments for me as well. When Max was five, Emily and I took him to a local mall in Florida. The mistake was choosing to do it late on a Saturday afternoon. Just when Max was fascinated by a toy in a store and oblivious to anything else, the loud-speaker announced that the mall would be closing in twenty minutes. Emily knew how tough it was to move Max, and I could envision spending a night locked away in a shopping mall. Just trying to move him gently toward the door, as Emily could do so skillfully, set him off that day. Emily and I then each took a hand and started walking.

It was a disaster. The more I tugged and pulled, the louder he screamed. I imagined the shoppers passing by and glancing at us, maybe recognizing me and assuming we were beating this child. Then Max went flat on the floor. There was nothing to do but physically pull him toward the exit. I tried to avoid the stares of the passers-by for fear they would call the mall police. We made it through the doors just as the guards were locking up, and Max finished his tantrum, thankfully, outside.

Then there was the occasion at home when, while we were finishing dinner and Max was watching TV in the next room, we heard a loud crash. We ran only to discover that Max had hurled a beautiful vase that Patty and I brought back from Korea. When it smashed against the floor Max fell into a tantrum. I marveled at the way Emily was able to calm him gently. It still didn't replace the vase, but things like that aren't as important as we think at the time.

But some of the times were terrifying. Like the night we were eating dinner at a round, glass-topped wicker table in the family room. Max was six and hyperactive. As always, Max quaffed his dinner down and began fidgeting while the rest of us tried to finish with some semblance of grace. Before I could comprehend what was happening, he put both feet firmly on the base of the table and shoved back with such brute force that the chair instantly tipped backward, hurtling Max to the tile floor. It sounded like a train wreck. We leapt out of our chairs, thinking of calling 911, because no one could escape this without a concussion. By the time I got around the table, Patty and Emily were already kneeling beside Max. I saw him, still cradled in the now broken wicker chair, eyes closed, and a peaceful expression on his face. My heart sank. Then he simply opened his eyes, smiled, and said in the most audible words he'd ever uttered, "Whoa! It's a long way down!"

When the shock wore off and our hearts stopped racing, we couldn't help bursting into laughter. To this day, Patty and I will jokingly say, "Whoa! It's a long way down!"

But even in our most difficult moments, we could see Max loving others in an extraordinary way. Like the time when we delivered the Angel Tree gifts. Or the time when one of us was sick and Max would simply stand quietly beside us, as if he was sharing our suffering. And never once did Patty or I see Emily's loving commitment waver. She would stay calm. Always. Both Emily and Max seemed in the firm grip of God's loving hands.

Adjusting to Max's being with us was often hard for me to handle. I don't have time for all the demands made on me, and I feel under constant stress; I'm at the top of the type-A scale. So I've had little time for the normal things of life, like getting on the floor and building Legos with a young, very active child who can only communicate with excited gestures or tugs on the arm or an occasional outburst. In the early days, I thought to myself, *I'm not wired for this.*

I soon learned. Max stopped me cold. To him I'm not a public figure or a big-time so-called Christian celebrity. And surprising though it has been, I've grown to love becoming an ordinary grandfather. When Emily and Max come, I clear the decks. No writing, no BreakPoint broadcast recordings, no answering calls. Instead, we carefully lay out the schedule for the week, which becomes locked in cement — or more correctly, locked in Max's mind, which is just as hard. He simply can't understand changes to schedules. So when it comes time to visit the Naples Zoo and surrounding gardens, always near the top of Max's list, Max, Emily, and I walk the same familiar pathways, see the same beautiful flora and fauna, and ogle the same animals, including the fierce-looking alligators who surface uncomfortably close to the banks of the lake's waters. Now I'm not one to keep visiting a tourist attraction, but no matter how often Max visits, we go back and back. For me it's turned out to be fun, in part because I vicariously experience Max's joy, watching him skip along the path, looking for the banana tree. He loves bananas.

Watching Emily with Max has taught me a powerful lesson about relationships. She finds a way to get inside Max's mind, to think as he thinks, which enables her to help him make sense out of life. I've watched Emily do this with her drawings they call Picture Talks. Even when Max was much younger and in the midst of a violent eruption, Emily would sit beside him, lovingly holding his trembling shoulders. And with nothing but a pen and paper and her gentle, probing questions, she could bring him back to balance. I've seen Emily do this with Max for as little as ten minutes, for as long as an hour.

I spend much of my life trying to do this same thing, not to a screaming child but to mature Christians studying biblical worldview. This isn't arcane philosophy; it's the nuts and bolts of life, helping us make sense of things in a confusing and fast-moving world. I've learned almost as much about teaching by watching Emily and Max as I have studying great books.

Learning to get inside Max's mind, to see the world as he does, is painstaking. But it has helped with my impatience, a fault those around me frequently remind me of. I've prayed often for patience, but it was Max who did the job, perhaps not completely if you ask those close to me. But I'm getting better.

I've certainly learned to be more understanding of others. To be honest, I've often been harsh in judgments about other people.

I hated, for example, to sit on a crowded airplane with kids nearby screaming for two hours when I was trying to read or work. I would ask myself, *How could a parent allow that?* Amidst my grumbles I would occasionally stare sternly at the guilty parent. Now, instead, I think of Max and Emily; my first thought is maybe that child has special needs. Instead of getting angry, I find I can read and study and work right through the volcanic eruptions taking place two rows behind me. And I go out of my way to be kind to the parents involved.

Seeing life this way has helped me at home. All husbands and wives have their tense moments, but now I find myself thinking more often that maybe Patty has a good reason for saying what she said or for getting irritated at me. (And she's usually right.)

I always thought I was caring for others. When I was in the White House, every Christmas I went into the basement telephone center to hand out chocolates and thank the switchboard operators who were so helpful during the year. But now I question my motives. Did I do it so that I could say I was the only White House assistant who did? Just as in all these years of ministry visiting prisoners, loving the unlovable, embracing dying AIDS victims, counseling angry, hurting people, I was doing what I knew God called me to do. But was I caring because people expected me to do this? Or was my heart truly broken for them? Once, on a Habitat for Humanity project in Chicago with former president Jimmy Carter, we were housed in a dreadful tenement. I found myself awake for hours, with sirens piercing the night air. I couldn't wait for it to be over, because I knew I could then get back to my own bed and clean sheets. I was convicted then that I really wasn't able to share in their sufferings, really see life through their eyes. Max and Emily have taught me a lot about caring with compassion, though I still have a long way to go.

MAX HAS HAD A DRAMATIC, TRANSFORMING EFFECT on our whole family. I confess now that in the early years when Max and Emily came to Florida, Patty and I were sometimes fearful. We knew it meant meltdowns and anxiety. We walked around the house as if we were about to trip an invisible wire setting off a landmine.

I remember when our fears and apprehensions left us. Max was in his early teens. Patty and I were standing in the airport terminal waiting for Emily and Max to arrive for a visit. We were straining our eyes to find them in the stream of passengers. When we spotted them, instead of Max staring vacantly in all directions, he seemed to be peering intently ahead, looking for us. As soon as he saw us, he broke free of Emily's grip and came running toward us with the biggest smile I'd ever seen on a kid's face. He was shouting, "Grandpa! Grandpa! Happy! Happy!" And then he threw his arms around each of us. And it has been that way ever since.

Max has had a similar effect on others and has, in part, been responsible for bringing our family even closer together. Our other grandchildren go out of their way to make Max feel comfortable and to focus attention on him. The stereotype of teenagers looking out only for themselves has decidedly not been our experience.

Our oldest son, Wendell, lives near Emily, and though he's incredibly busy with his own children and business, he has always been there for Max. One prized possession is a photograph of Wendell teaching Max how to tighten a screw through a piece of wood. Max has his lip turned just so, intently following his uncle, as together they rescued the leather seats from an old Audi we'd driven and given to Emily. It was headed for the junkyard, but Max couldn't bear to part with the seats. So thanks to Wendell, Max has two Audi seats he sits on in the living room, which may be the only living room in America so decorated.

During one family reunion Wendell and his brother, Chris, who lives in South Carolina, took Max tubing. The tube was tied to a small dinghy with a thirty-horsepower motor. Chris helped Max climb on and steady his body across the tube, at the very location used to film the movie *Jaws*. Though Emily started shaking visibly at the sight of her child going to sea on a big rubber inner tube, the boys took him out, making large circles in the sea, perhaps a hundred yards off the beach. Max's hair was blowing straight back, spray hitting his face and his eyes wide as saucers. Emily was running up and down the beach with her camera, getting pictures and, of course, watching for a dorsal fin. Max beamed each time he passed those of us on the shore. He couldn't wave or he'd be thrown off, but you could tell by the look on his face he was saying, "Look at me, Ma; look at me, Grandpa!"

I've seen Max bring joy and love to others besides us, sometimes causing serious, grown men to act as if they were children again. Once when Max and Emily were visiting, we took them to see the family of Norma Wessner, whose late husband, Ken, had been one of my closest colleagues. Norma has a large condo, but it was packed with her daughter, Barbara, her son-in-law Ross, four grandchildren, and one of their spouses. We were hesitant because crowds, noise, and meeting new people can sometimes set Max off.

I said an extra prayer under my breath as Norma welcomed us. I had Max by the hand, carefully introducing him to each of the family members. Norma's son-in-law Ross is a doctor, very serious and very professional; and his son is also a doctor, then in residence, also serious and professional. When we went into the living room, Emily sat with her arm around Max. He remained quiet, staring warily at all the new faces. I breathed a sigh of relief.

It didn't last. Within minutes, Max bounced off the sofa, stood in the middle of the room and said, "Let's see the vacuums. Where are the vacuums?" Vacuums fascinate Max, like bananas and car seats. As Ross brought them out — three in all — Max was squealing with joy and shouting instructions: "Turn it on! Turn it off!"

Soon, both doctor Andersons, the senior in his midfifties, the son in his late twenties, were whisking over the carpets with vacuums roaring at full power. Max, beads of sweat dripping from his brow, jumped up and down in perfect bliss. The adults were soon shouting for joy along with him.

Maybe providentially this day prepared the Andersons for things to come. Two years later, their daughter married a man who was a single dad with an autistic child exactly Max's age.

Children like Max can be disruptive. So why is it that these same kids so often bring such joy to people? Emily and I may have discovered one answer. I realized the attraction of Max and others like him during that magnificent moment when I baptized him in our swimming pool. When I looked intently into his eyes, I spoke the words of the baptismal declaration, "In the name of the Father, the Son, and the Holy Spirit, I baptize you ..." Max's expression was one of total and joyous acceptance. His countenance displayed the simple, childlike faith Jesus spoke of (Matthew 18:4).

Another reason for Max's appeal is his honesty. While Max doesn't understand how the world works — and therefore isn't free to do all the things most people take for granted — he is completely free in the area that holds most of us captive. Max truly sees the world more as God intended — he's not judgmental or impressed by looks, status, or finances. He doesn't try to "fit in." He never boasts, and Emily says he can't lie. Actually, she said he tried twice but failed. Ironically, lying would signify a developmental advancement in his thinking. Max puts on no pretensions, and there is no malice, deceit, hypocrisy, envy, or slander, as the Scripture tells us to avoid. Max is simply incapable of pretending to like someone to get something from them. He loves the things he loves just because he loves them, not because someone else thinks he ought to.

Most people are accustomed to being rewarded for their deeds. But God puts priority on the things of the Spirit, which turn out to be the things that Max does without even trying.

Could it be that though we are all fallen — "There is no one righteous, not even one" (Roman 3:10) — some people are not as affected by the fall as others? And those who aren't give us a glimpse of what God intended for his original creation. One quality might be exceptional cognitive abilities, like Dustin Hoffman's character in the movie *Rain Man* who could do elaborate calculations in his head — or Max's ability to memorize. Some people in Max's situation have uncanny musical or artistic abilities, or the ability to have joyous communion with God, undistracted by the world's temptations — abilities often limited by the fall. This characteristic gives the disabled an almost prophetic role. As one theologian wrote, "Their lives embody the wisdom of God in ways that interrogate, critique, and undermine the status quo."*

This helps explain why so many non-Christians are drawn to helping disabled youngsters. At Max's special-needs activities, I've been inspired by the volunteers who joyously give themselves to these kids. One afternoon at a basketball game — you can't really call it that since no one keeps score — I studied the volunteers. Young high school students, as well as many moms and dads, were teaching these kids to dribble, pass a ball, and in some cases lifting their hands to show them how to sink a basket. Helping them gives such joy.

But something didn't square when I first watched these games. A secularist or even a nominal Christian probably believes what he's been taught in school, that humans are mature apes, who came originally from a single plant cell in the primordial soup. So to help the weak is absolutely counterintuitive. Darwinian evolution teaches the survival of the fittest; if this is so, the ultimate ethical pursuit is survival. The faster the weak are institutionalized or swept out of sight or otherwise eliminated, the better for you, so long as you are among the strong, that is. Yet even so-called naturalists, who believe in random evolution, seem to go out of their way to help the weak. I believe that the image of God is in all humans, so we see something special in these people and are drawn to them, even against our own worldview.

But the committed Darwinian naturalist refuses to acknowledge this. Princeton professor Peter Singer teaches packed lecture halls

---

*Amos Yong, *Theology and Down Syndrome: Reimagining Disability in Late Modernity* (Waco, Texas: Baylor University Press, 2007).

what is called utilitarianism, that is, the goal of society is to maximize happiness, doing the greatest good for the greatest number. That's why he favors infanticide for the disabled or unfit (if they aren't weeded out in the womb) and terminating care for those with Alzheimer's or others inconsiderate enough to use scarce resources for a long, slow, natural death. His positions, though we may be repulsed by them, are the only logical ethical framework for a post-Christian, naturalistic society, particularly one with ever scarcer and more expensive medical resources.

This is why, in a much ballyhooed debate on the Princeton campus with Singer, the late Harriet McBride Johnson, a severely handicapped and brilliant disabilities-rights advocate, failed so badly. One of her arguments was that caregivers get great joy out of helping the handicapped. Singer couldn't imagine why Johnson, an atheist like he is, could even argue this. By responding that there is no such thing as altruism, only self-interest, he rebutted her argument handily.

But there *is* altruism — which atheism can't explain. I've seen it in the faces and actions of those dedicated teachers in Max's school, in the actions of most people who come in contact with Max. Altruism has to be wired into us by God, which is why Atheism is irrational.

ALL OF US WANT TO BE ROLE MODELS for our kids and grandkids. When I taught Max to wax the car — a big day in both of our lives — I watched him imitate every single move I made, including standing back, taking an extra breath, and admiring our handiwork. To this day he is proud he did that — and he loves to wax people's cars. Now when he visits, it's on his to-do list.

Whenever Max arrives at our house he skips through the rooms taking inventory to make sure nothing has been moved since his last visit. He finds security and comfort in routines and familiar surroundings. One place he almost always stops is my ego wall — yes, I admit I have one — where there are pictures of me with various luminaries collected over the years. Max stands at that wall and rattles off the names of the people I'm pictured with. "Grandpa and President Bush ... Grandpa and the pope ... Grandpa and Billy Graham ..." And on and on he goes through every picture on the wall.

We have placed one restriction on Max, however: he is never to touch the switches for the ceiling fans. The reason is simple. He is obsessed with motors and household appliances. If he were to turn the fan on and off several times in rapid sequence it would burn out the motor. He knows that it's Grandpa's job to turn on the fans.

When Max returned to school after a visit, one of his teachers asked him to tell his class about his trip to Florida. He immediately recited all the pictures on the wall. The teacher called Emily to ask if Max was making this up — did her father really know all those people? Emily explained that I had served in the White House. So the next day they questioned Max standing in the front of the class: "What was your grandfather's job at the White House?"

Max quickly responded, "He turned on the fans."

MAX FORCES US TO RAISE THE MOST IMPORTANT QUESTION of our age: What does it mean to be human? If the geneticists and "science for science's sake" crowd were to have their way, we would weed out the unfit and create the perfect human race by infanticide, euthanasia, or, eventually, genetic engineering.

But what would happen to our humanity? Gone would be many of the problems and ailments — that's true. But also gone would be the trials that shape our character — and inevitably our freedom would disappear. For to be perfect and live problem-free in a fallen world is to be a slave to whomever makes you that way. And if we, as creatures, were perfectly programmed by our genes, we would be stripped of the capacity for genuine love, which by its very definition must be an act of free will. Love goes to the very essence of being a Christian, indeed of being human.

The understanding of what love really is, and how God uses adversity to bring us to this point, is the great lesson that Emily and our whole family have learned through these experiences. Real love is refined through pain and suffering, which is why one friend, when she learned of Max's autism, said to me, "Oh, you have found favor from God, because he has given you this special-needs child so you can experience sacrificial love." I didn't fully understand at first, but over the years have found these words to be true.

Most people think they know about love from their parents or their families or from close friends. Christians believe they have experienced love supremely in their encounter with God. Certainly I did, when I was in my friend's driveway in August 1973. Having for the first time truly heard the gospel, I cried out to God, surrendering my life to him. In the years since, I've been overwhelmed with gratitude for his love, forgiving my sins. It has driven me through nearly four decades of prison ministry loving those the world calls unlovable. I even dared write a book entitled *Loving God*, which should have made me an expert.

But when it comes to loving God and others — I mean really loving — I now realize how far short I have fallen. As hard as it has been to watch our only daughter face such obstacles, we have witnessed God using Max to deepen Emily's faith. And we've come to understand one of the most profound truths of Christianity: the object of our faith is to love.

Emily has, in a sense, incarnated God's love. From the time she fell in love with Max when he was two weeks old until today, her love has never wavered. She has sacrificed — though she doesn't call it that — everything that could stand in the way of her giving as full a life as possible to Max. Emily is a talented artist and has done some part-time work; she could have done much more, but it would have taken time away from Max. And when threatened by school officials who wanted to force him into a boarding school, she seriously contemplated fleeing the state to escape the court's jurisdiction.

She's been through deep waters health-wise as well, with a malignant melanoma removed surgically some years ago. And just as we started this book she contracted a rare superbug from an overdose of antibiotics. She was in great physical distress for almost a year but worked her way through it and never failed to care for Max's needs. And as hard as it may be to believe, in all these years I have seldom seen her discouraged or depressed. Whenever she has heard me call her "heroic," she cringes. "No! No," she says. "It is a blessing!" I've discovered she really means it.

The only possible explanation is that God's grace has poured through Emily, enabling her to give love selflessly. Her devotion is the kind that Jesus spoke of when he said, "Greater love has no one than this, that he lay down his life for his friends" (John 15:13).

Most of us never think of loving this way: a literal sacrifice of oneself. When I was in the Marines I always wondered if I would have the courage (it's really love) to hurl myself on a grenade to save my men. I'm glad I was never tested. For despite all the bravado, I, like most people, probably wouldn't have done it. But this is the ultimate test of love. Emily is fortunate to have been tested and, sinful nature though she has, passed the test.

In my thirty-seven years as a Christian, I've only personally experienced one other example of this kind of love. During the seven months I spent in prison I absorbed some tough blows; my dad died the second month I was in prison. Later on I discovered that I had lost my law license in Virginia. After that, one of the Watergate judges cut the sentences short of the other Watergate offenders while the judge who sentenced me refused all entreaties. But the toughest part of it all was that I had problems within my family where I was really needed; I had never felt more helpless. Then senior congressman Al Quie, a member of the Bible study group that embraced me upon my conversion, called to tell me he was going to see President Ford to ask if he could serve the rest of my prison sentence so I could be home with my family. He meant it.

That night I knelt at my bunk and thanked God I was in prison, because I now knew beyond any doubt that Christ was exactly who he said he was. Nothing less could have caused a man to sacrifice himself as Al Quie was willing to do. And I've never doubted the reality of Christ from that day to this. (As it worked out, Al didn't have to do it; I was released by the judge three days after his call.)

What does Jesus mean when he says, "Greater love has no one than this …"? What is the love that Paul refers to as the greatest good, even greater than faith or hope or anything else? What kind of love motivated Al and motivates Emily?

The word *love* in English is inadequate, often confusing. The Bible writers draw on the Greek vocabulary, which contains four words to define love. Three of these are subjective: *eros*, for romantic love; *storje*, for mere affection; and *phila*, for friendship. The one objective type of love is the fourth, *agape*, which refers to God's love, complete and unconditional devotion, willing the highest possible good for another. Reason might tell us that we only give love when it is deserved or when we calculate it has some worth to us or meets some need. *Agape* says no; love itself is the denial of self and love for others in its purest form. This is the ultimate Good of life.

God is *agape* love in his very nature. He is three persons, Father, Son, and Holy Spirit, in a continuous self-loving relationship, which our souls will one day share.

Since the object of faith is love, our personal goal should be to experience *agape* love in the flesh. But can we fallen humans achieve that? Probably not in this life. At best we can work toward it, approximate it, or get glimpses of it.

Have you ever wondered why some Christians seem preternaturally peaceful, always giving others the benefit of the doubt, ignoring the slings and arrows of life, generously and inconspicuously helping others, humble, unaffected by praise? They have discovered some measure of *agape* love. It is what I have finally gotten into my head after thirty-seven years as a believer; and it has been life-changing. I find myself now consciously, as best as an imperfect person can, trying to practice *agape* love. When I do this I discover some amazing consequences. Old grudges disappear, and I'm actually incapable of hate — and even feel sorry for those who may have betrayed me in human terms.

Not that I can maintain this disposition consistently; it's a daily struggle, just as Paul has described it in his life. But when I can do this, I experience perfect peace and a glimpse of the glory to come. Love — the kind we seek as Christians, the kind my daughter Emily emulates — is the cement that holds the universe together. A power stronger than the mightiest empires, it invariably triumphs over evil. It is irresistible. It is the objective, ultimate Good.

Isn't it just like God, that after all these years of study and service as a Christian, I would experience this ultimate Good — or as close to it as humans can — in the lives of my daughter and grandson?

Emily heroic? No. She has simply found the greatest joy in life. Max disabled? No. The world labels him such, but I think Peppermint Patti got it right; he is an incalculable gift from God. And a gift to me personally.

Emily and Max's life together has been a dance. And I, awkward though I am on the dance floor, join them eagerly, dancing with my grandson and my precious daughter as if she were six years old again.

THANK YOU ...

A few years ago the impulse to write these stories gripped my life with such force that I dropped everything — except, of course, the oversized cup of coffee in my hand. I knew that God had written his story all over our lives. And thankfully, when it came time to put it on paper, he wrote his story all over this book. For this, for all of it, I am amazed and grateful.

It has been a privilege to write this book with my dad. Thank you, Dad, for sharing your most personal stories and for bringing vision, structural expertise, and tough editing skills to this book. More importantly, thank you for being a loving father and grandfather. And it was my stepmother Patty's idea that my dad and I should write together. She even came up with the title. But our story exists because of the love and support of my entire family: Mom, Dad, Patty, Wendell, Joanne, Chris, Cheryll, Stephanie, Rebecca, Charlie, Caroline, and a big welcome to Heather and Grant. And, of course, beautiful Max.

Many thanks go to the wonderful people at Zondervan. I salute the bravery of Dudley Delffs, my publisher, who took a chance on a visual artist. And I bow to the indispensable John Sloan — editor, visionary, mentor, and friend — who helped me find my voice. John's guidance and encouragement helped me feel brave, which is exactly what I hope this book will do for the reader. And my thanks to Bob Hudson, the second editor of this book, who lassoed all my wild apostrophes, hogtied a few sentences, and studied the contents through hawk-eyes. Thank you to the marketing, promotional, and production teams — Don Gates, Karen Campbell, T. J. Rathbun, Matt Saganski, Brad Hill, Jeff Gifford, Michelle Lenger, Curt Diepenhorst, Beth Shagene, Joyce Ondersma, and everyone behind the scenes.

Thank you to all who have generously permitted me to share your stories in this book. To Sherrie Irvin, for turning my dad's creative penmanship into neatly typed pages. To my mom, Nancy, for teaching me about joy, for giving us all the cardboard we ever wanted as kids, and for reading this manuscript and knowing when it's best to simply smile ... and correct grammar. To Lena, for ten amazing years of teaching Max, for filling our home with sunshine, and for taking Max on adventures when I needed to write. To Sue, for telling me, "Keep writing." Everyone needs a friend like you. To my first readers — Sue, Ayn, Paul, Gigi, and Becky — your input has been invaluable. Thanks to all who have prayed for us and for this project. And to Chris and Susan, for thirty years of friendship and for always, no matter what, making me laugh.

I am thankful for Peppermint Patti, for her words, and her witness.

My deepest gratitude to the miracle workers at Melmark New England, to Jim for keeping Max safe, to our friends at the ARC and CAR and DDS. Thank you to all the teachers and volunteers who over the years have given selflessly to Max, with an extra wink to Wendy. A special thank you to all the parents of extraordinary children who inspire me daily. And my thanks to every stranger who has shown us kindness, and to every storeowner who has allowed Max to vacuum, organize the refrigerators, and redesign the banana displays ... again. We are blessed with friends who have cheered us on and a church that loves us just as we are.

And to the girl in my high school, oh brave dear one, who asked me what kind of life I wanted to have ...

Share Your Thoughts

With the Author: Your comments will be forwarded to the author when you send them to *zauthor@zondervan.com*.

With Zondervan: Submit your review of this book by writing to *zreview@zondervan.com*.

Free Online Resources at
www.zondervan.com

Zondervan AuthorTracker: Be notified whenever your favorite authors publish new books, go on tour, or post an update about what's happening in their lives at www.zondervan.com/authortracker.

Daily Bible Verses and Devotions: Enrich your life with daily Bible verses or devotions that help you start every morning focused on God. Visit www.zondervan.com/newsletters.

Free Email Publications: Sign up for newsletters on Christian living, academic resources, church ministry, fiction, children's resources, and more. Visit www.zondervan.com/newsletters.

Zondervan Bible Search: Find and compare Bible passages in a variety of translations at www.zondervanbiblesearch.com.

Other Benefits: Register yourself to receive online benefits like coupons and special offers, or to participate in research.

ZONDERVAN®

ZONDERVAN.com/
AUTHORTRACKER
follow your favorite authors